You Are Psychic!

OTHER BOOKS BY PETE A. SANDERS, JR.

Introduction to the Concepts of Being a Free Soul
The Dynamics of Being a Free Soul
(course book and cassettes)

· You Are ·
Psychic!

The Free Soul Method

Pete A. Sanders, Jr.

Fawcett Columbine • New York

A Fawcett Columbine Book
Published by Ballantine Books
Copyright © 1989 by Pete A. Sanders, Jr.

All rights reserved under International and Pan-American Copyright Conventions. Published in the United States by Ballantine Books, a division of Random House, Inc., New York, and distributed in Canada by Random House of Canada Limited, Toronto.
http://www.randomhouse.com
Library of Congress Catalog Card Number: 89-91511

ISBN: 0-449-90507-1

This edition published by arrangement with Rawson Associates, an imprint of Macmillan Publishing Company, New York.

Text illustrations by Dorothe Cavanagh

Manufactured in the United States of America

First Ballantine Books Edition: June 1990

20 19 18 17 16 15 14 13 12

This book is dedicated to that part of each of us that knows we are unlimited and strives to explore our full potentials and freedoms

The important thing is not to stop questioning.

ALBERT EINSTEIN

Always bear in mind that your own resolution to succeed is more important than any one thing.

ABRAHAM LINCOLN

Self-conquest is the greatest of all victories.

PLATO

Acknowledgments

FIRST AND FOREMOST to the many Free Soul instructors and students who contributed their personal experiences and support during the preparation of the book. Without their openness and candor the project in its final form would not have been possible.

To my wife, Debbie, for standing by me both in the early struggling years and later during the stresses and pressures of travel and growing demands on my time.

My deepest thanks also to the following special people who helped make it possible for a larger segment of the public to receive the techniques and methods that have been my life's work:

To Sheila Tronn Cooper, my agent, for her unfailing enthusiasm from the first moment of our meeting. Her support has been irreplaceable.

To John Diamond for the many hours of wise counsel he

has provided both legally and as a friend. His presence has truly been a blessing to my life.

To Eleanor Rawson of Rawson Associates for having the vision to get these breakthroughs to the public, and for setting the highest literary standards and helping me to achieve them.

To Norman Lobsenz, an exceptionally knowledgeable editor, for his assistance in the final preparation of the text, as well as his literary objectivity in its review.

To Dorothe Cavanagh, the illustrator and painter, for her accurate and artistic representations of the four Psychic Reception Areas.

To Margaret Pinyan, my literary assistant and word processor *extraordinaire*, for her years of input and editing help from the very first draft to the final printing.

To Mary Kendzierski, my personal assistant, for her years of loyal service and also her initial assistance with depicting the Psychic Reception Areas.

Also, a special thanks to the following Free Soul senior instructors featured in the book, both for their contributions and for their years of hard work and sincere dedication to Free Soul's principles of showing others how to be their own teachers: Eddy Cettina, John Duker, Gerry Eitner, Elaine Gibbs, Ali Habib, Gail Johnston, Sue Leonard, Scott Maley, Fran Mandell, Mimi Miller, Kathy Neal, Luce Neyra, Terry Padilla, David Pierce, Ann Stacy Russell, Marlene Shiple, Marybeth Spain, Marianne Stanley, Carol Swersky, and Barbara West.

Contents

Preface
Before You Read This
Book

IF EVER you wished you could reach beyond the everyday world and experience virtually limitless knowledge and control of your destiny, the time for merely wishing is over. If ever you dreamed of being able to tap psychic insight and wisdom whenever you need it, the time for just dreaming is over.

The skills for achieving those goals are now within your grasp.

Imagine what it would be like to wake each morning knowing what the day holds in store for you—being able to sense in advance the moods of the people you will be with, to take exactly those steps that will help you be successful in all that you do.

That power can be yours. By the time you finish reading this book the capacity to assess other people's temperaments and personalities, and the ability to sense, feel, hear, and see events before they happen can become everyday skills for you.

That is, I know, a startling claim. But during my years of biomedical chemistry and brain science study at Massachusetts Institute of Technology (MIT), I discovered basic principles and training techniques that make these psychic abilities available to anyone who wants them. Later, I refined and successfully tested those methods around the world. I have taught them to thousands of men and women. Now, in this book, I will share them with you.

No longer need you be limited to merely talking about the idea of extrasensory perception, or to marveling at random psychic experiences others have, or to seeking help or counsel from a few naturally gifted persons who are labeled "psychics." The psychic world is real, and you can be a part of it.

The freedom to explore your higher ESP potentials is not only your birthright but the most important of your personal liberties. Knowing how to use those potentials in practical ways—how to tap on demand the psychic abilities heretofore locked within yourself—will provide you with life-changing and life-enhancing opportunities.

The right to explore and develop your psychic talents, and to apply them to your daily life, has been suppressed for thousands of years. Superstition and dogma, ridicule and cynicism, have combined to shroud ESP and what have come to be called "paranormal" abilities in a veil of fear, mystery, and misunderstanding. The myth that ESP is limited to a few "psychics" or to only random, uncontrollable experiences has barred the door to the greatest of human adventures.

Despite these obstacles, belief in the existence of paranormal abilities and ESP phenomena has managed to flourish. A recent University of Chicago survey reported that 67 percent of those queried—two out of every three persons—claimed to have had a psychic experience. I believe that 100 percent of us are psychic and capable of using our ESP at will as easily as we blink our eyes or think a thought.

Consider that we live in an age when most leading physicists accept the existence of realms of phenomena beyond the three dimensions of our physical environment. Scientists who are proponents of the new "Superstring Theory" of subatomic physics believe that all matter—including human beings—exists in ten dimensions, and that all matter and energy may be able to "communicate" at subatomic levels.

You, too, possess the power of unlimited communication. It exists in your mind—your personal highly sophisticated internal receiver and transmitter. Most of us use only about 10 percent of its vast capacity; the other 90 percent of its power goes virtually untapped.

The goal of this book is to show you how to tap fully the limitless energy of your mind and break through into the dimensions beyond. I know you can achieve this because I have done so myself, and have helped thousands of others to do so. Let me take you back, for a few moments, to the beginnings of my personal belief in ESP, and to the start of my search for ways to use it for a better and more fulfilling life.

My Psychic Awakening

As a child, I was fascinated by the original television program on ESP entitled *Alcoa Presents* (it was later renamed *One Step Beyond*). Each week it dramatized a factual story having to do with a paranormal experience. I still recall one tale of psychic communication over vast distances, another recounting premonitions of the sinking of the *Titanic,* and still another of a dream that forewarned a man of a physical danger. As a result, I came to believe that the extrasensory world was real—but mistakenly I thought that only those with special gifts could access it, or that it could only be experienced by chance.

That belief in ESP was strengthened in my youth when my

widowed mother, Aurora, in her search for spiritual suste-
nance, took me along as she visited a wide range of psychics
and mystics.

Time and again I heard information presented that could
not be known to or obtained by the physical senses. Although
most of the psychics claimed to be gifted since birth, they at
least had seemed to find a way to control their ESP. If they
could learn, I reasoned, it must be possible for anyone to be
psychic, even someone like myself who had shown no automatic or "natural" paranormal abilities. My reasoning proved
correct.

My first personal psychic experience occurred several
years later when I was fifteen. My mother had invited a
quirky old psychic (call him Sam) to teach a group of us how
to see an aura, the energy field that surrounds our body and
manifests itself as a "halo" of varicolored light. Sam's clothes
were disheveled and he fidgeted constantly, but he professed
to know everything there was to know about Aura Vision. In
truth, he was adept at it and could see auras at will. That
night he was going to share his secrets with us.

Sam told us to relax our vision as we looked at Cecile, the
"aura model" for the evening. Sam then instructed us to
notice the places on our own body where we felt an itch,
and then look at those same places on Cecile's body to see
what we observed there. I thought this was the most ridiculous approach to Aura Vision I had ever heard! I was sure this
weird method couldn't possibly work, so I didn't try at all. I
just relaxed and went along with it.

To my surprise, I suddenly saw Cecile's aura. Around her
head were brilliant light blues with flashes of dark red;
around her body the aura was a dull gray, with two dark scar-
like lines across the area of the abdomen where I had felt an
itch just moments before. Afterward Sam explained that the
blue light around Cecile's head represented her basic calm
personality, and the red flashes represented her tendency to
give way at times to explosions of temper. She had also had
two recent abdominal operations.

For me the experience proved that auras did indeed exist, though "itching" did not strike me as the best technique for discerning them. Only two others in our group saw anything of Cecile's aura. I felt that, in my case, the very ridiculousness of Sam's method had prevented me from trying too hard, and as a result I was truly relaxed. It was that totally relaxed state, I believe, that first allowed my psychic vision to unfold. I soon learned to discard the gimmick of itching and just relax naturally to open my "third eye."

The Psychic Marketplace

Growing up in Southern California, I had the chance to see every type of psychic imaginable. Those experiences in the psychic marketplace convinced me that while some psychics were gifted and sincere, others clearly exaggerated their abilities. I recall one California woman—let's call her Helen—whose psychic reputation was so widespread that she and her husband held nightly sessions for different groups all over the state. At these meetings Helen would "open a channel" to a spirit guide she called Tomar, and through him answer questions and deliver messages.

I was struck by the way Helen's aura varied as she answered different queries. For example, one woman said she felt her husband was troubled but she could not communicate with him. "How do I get him to talk to me about what's bothering him?" the woman asked.

Helen easily and confidently channeled information and advice (which the questioner later reported was accurate and worked effectively), and while she did so her aura remained solid, wide, and bright. But when another woman asked a question about a possible career change, Helen's aura faded and shrank. It seemed as if she was unable to respond. I expected Helen then to say something like, "I'm drawing a blank on that, so perhaps you need to make your own decision." Instead, Helen gave the woman specific advice on what job to look for, and even the recommendation to move to a different city. This time while she was speaking her aura remained narrow and dull. I was startled by the difference, but since I was new at seeing auras I said nothing. (Later I learned that the woman did move, with disastrous results: she spent nine months unemployed and looking for a job that never materialized.)

When I asked others in the group about it later, they all said they had either seen no aura or noticed no change. With no evident psychic ability of their own, these people simply placed total faith in Helen, whom they believed to be "gifted." Most of them went to other psychics as well and relied totally on their answers to their questions.

The saddest thing about all this, I realized, was the circle of psychic dependency that enclosed both the psychics and their clients. Helen at one time described aspects of my life she could not have known without ESP, and I knew she was extremely psychically open. The answers she gave when her aura was bright proved to be accurate. But those she gave when her aura was dimmed proved flawed, and I believe Helen knew they were flawed. She was just as ensnared in the trap of psychic dependency as her clients.

What I mean is this: People who do not know that they have or can develop their psychic abilities place the burden of tremendous expectations on the Helens of the world, the persons they believe can use ESP to help them. The pressure of those expectations no doubt led Helen to exaggerate her natural psychic talents. In the process, everyone lost.

Over the years, what stayed in my mind about this and similar examples of psychic dependency and expectations was the fact that there were so many people eager for information about the psychic world. I believed these people deserved better than the false gurus, commercial rip-offs, or outright charlatans who so often seem to dominate the psychic marketplace. I believed that reliable knowledge of the extrasensory world—and practical methods for obtaining it—should be made available to everyone. You shouldn't have to depend on someone else to "be psychic" for you! *You should be able to be your own free soul!* I headed off to college looking for scientific ways to make that desire a reality.

What Is Free Soul, and How Did It Start?

Although as a premedical student at MIT I studied the basic "hard" sciences such as biology, chemistry, and biochemistry, I found my true niche in the psychology department. There I immersed myself in courses and laboratory work on physiological psychology and brain science. In simpler terms, I studied the human brain and the senses—all that we know about them and all of their yet untapped and unlimited capabilities.

When I graduated from MIT, I was accepted to attend Harvard Medical School. But after much soul-searching I declined the offer and decided to follow a different career path.

At MIT, as you will see in the next chapter, I had uncovered principles and techniques I believed could help put the psychic ability that lies dormant within all of us into anyone's grasp. I knew there was a greater need for responsible work in that field than in the field of traditional medicine. I felt I could touch and enhance more lives by providing this type of service. I believed that individuals who search for psychic development have a right to learn without having to pay large sums of money or joining a cult. My goal was to find a way to make inexpensive, nondenominational psychic education widely available. In 1980, after traveling to many parts of the world to test my theories and techniques in a variety of environments and cultures, I achieved that goal by found-

ing Free Soul. It is a nonprofit organization that makes available revolutionary self-teaching techniques for developing
extrasensory talents and expanding the human potential.
Free Soul currently has hundreds of instructors who offer
classes throughout the U.S., as well as cassette courses and
textbooks. (For further information, write Free Soul, P.O. Box
1762, Sedona, Arizona 86339.)

There is no doubt that psychic potential exists. The question is, Are you going to develop that higher potential for
yourself, or allow it to remain blocked and unused? The
answer lies in this book. It contains the fundamental elements
of Free Soul's teachings, along with self-discovery exercises
and a wealth of personal experiences with psychic living. It
will show you how to unfold and fine-tune your own psychic
abilities.

Let me share with you a taste of what lies ahead. Chapter
1 tells the story of my discovery of the body's four Psychic
Reception Areas and the four psychic channels they open up
for you. Chapters 2 through 5 discuss in depth how to use
these four psychic senses. Each chapter also describes the
personality traits that accompany each specific psychic
strength. You will learn from this how best to deal with other
people, and how to gain new keys for career and personal
success.

Chapter 6 explores the world of the aura—how to sense
and interpret the body's energy field, and how to use your
new knowledge for your personal benefit. Chapters 7 and 8
take you beyond ordinary psychic sensitivity into even
higher potentials that can help you reduce stress, heal yourself, increase your creativity, and extend the boundaries of
consciousness beyond the three-dimensional world.

Chapter 9 is your gateway to tomorrow. With examples
from the experiences of Free Soul graduates, you will learn
how to expand your new-found psychic skills and take an
evolutionary step forward toward the control of your own
destiny.

The Frontier Ahead

When you answer the challenge of seeking your highest potential, the greatest journey of your life begins. Before you spreads the unlimited frontier of the mind, the psyche, and the soul. This journey into new territory is neither hazardous nor difficult. But it does require the courage to explore, to change, to grow. This book and the keys it contains will provide you with the foundation and support you need to make that journey a reality.

Know that what you seek from this book is possible; more important, know that learning how to find what you seek is invaluable. The wisdom you gain from that quest will give you more than knowledge. It will give you the freedom to be unlimited. *That is your birthright as a Free Soul.*

• 1 •

The Four Psychic Reception Areas

DO YOU REMEMBER the last time you were at a large cocktail party, or at a business convention where dozens of conversations were going on at the same time? With literally thousands of sound waves ricocheting around the room, you probably found the noise overwhelming.

But when you focused in their direction and listened more intently you were able to zero in on the person you were talking with or, if you wished, even pick up what someone far across the room was saying. That's a simple illustration of how selective focusing heightens your sensory abilities. Another is the way you stare when you want to see something more clearly. Staring "locks" the most sensitive part of the physical vision, the fovea of your eye, onto whatever you are looking at.

These common examples illustrate how using selective focusing with your five physical sense organs (eyes, ears, hands [as an aspect of the skin], tongue, and nose) helps sharpen your ability to see, hear, touch, taste, and smell when you want more information or greater detail. You use these focal points so naturally that you are seldom aware of what you are doing.

Similarly, the four psychic senses have focal points on or around your body that can increase and amplify your extrasensory abilities. I call them the "Psychic Reception Areas"— the locations for enhanced Psychic Feeling, Psychic Vision, Psychic Hearing, and Psychic Intuition. Just as physically focusing on your ears at that cocktail party helped you hear a particular conversation that was previously just background noise, so focusing on a Psychic Reception Area can open the way for you to experience psychic impressions with greater clarity.

Once you know the location of the Psychic Reception Areas and how to use them, you will be able to access your four psychic senses on command—that is, whenever you want to. In effect, you will be doubling the amount of information you receive about people, places, and events because you will be using nine senses (five physical and four psychic) instead of just five.

Think of what that can mean! Have you ever walked into a room after two people in it were arguing and felt that "the air was so thick you could cut it with a knife"? Of course you have. But arguments don't cause air molecules to become more dense. You were experiencing a psychic feeling. And what about all those times the phone rang and you knew who was calling before you answered? Psychic Intuition makes that possible. Wouldn't you like to be able to hear the truth about a product when a salesman is trying to sell you something? You can, with Psychic Hearing. And Psychic Vision can give you the advantage of being able to see the real truth reflected in a person's aura.

Until now you probably have been having experiences with ESP randomly. But this book will help you develop the ability to sense psychically *all* of the time. By learning to focus on the Psychic Reception Areas you will receive stronger psychic impressions—strong enough to divert your attention from your physical senses. With practice, even subtle energy patterns will be discernible. Best of all, you will be able to develop your extrasensory abilities safely and steadily. When you are able to turn them on at will you can also turn them off to prevent the possibility of a psychic overload. Additionally, you will have the increased security that greater awareness and skill always bring.

How the Psychic Senses Work

All our senses, physical and psychic, function in part by receiving and responding to some form of energy. Physical vision depends on the energy of light waves striking the eye. Physical hearing senses the vibrational energy of sound waves. Taste and smell function through chemical energy reactions between certain molecules and the receptor cells of the tongue and olfactory areas. The psychic senses follow a similar pattern, except that the energies they interact with cannot be discerned physically or measured by current technology.

That should not deter you from exploring your psychic ability. Many forms of energy affect your life whether you understand them or not. Two hundred years ago little was understood about electricity, but electric energy existed. Though scientifically unexplained, lightning struck, electric eels gave shocks, the nervous system functioned. Even today, you may not fully understand how electricity works although you use it routinely.

Consider what happens when you turn on a light. You don't need to understand how electrons travel back and forth in the wires. Neither do you need to be aware that for each of your thoughts and movements the electrical energy that is your brain and nervous system has processed millions of messages. You don't need to know that each of those brain messages involves billions of complex exchanges of chemical energy into electrical energy. Instead, you have learned by experience how to make those forms of energy work for you in practical ways even though you may not know *how* they work. You just raise your hand, flip the switch, and the light goes on.

You need to adopt the same approach to using your psychic senses. They receive the psychic energy that is emitted by all people, places, and objects. *Because you are energy, you can receive and identify those extrasensory vibrations.*

Much about the human brain is still unknown, and we use the word "mind" as a sort of shorthand to describe mental abilities that go beyond what we know about the physical wiring of the cortex. Brain scientists cannot yet explain exactly why or how we dream, how memory is structured, or how we form a creative thought. Yet every day we dream, we remember, and we think. Or consider the mystery of hypnosis. It has been studied and used successfully for over a century to reduce or eliminate pain (it has even been used in surgery instead of anesthesia), to help us control addictions, to uncover repressed memories—yet we still don't have a precise idea as to how or why hypnosis works.

The fact is that science today comprehends probably less than a tenth of what our brain and mind can do. In a world where many scientists now believe once unbelievable things—for instance, that all matter exists in ten dimensions; that time slows as you travel faster; that particles called tachyons, which can arrive at their destination before they leave their point of origin, may indeed exist; that the universe is literally a sea of interchangeable and interacting energy—in such a world the concept of psychic sensitivity, of ESP, is no longer a farfetched fantasy.

Therefore it is not reasonable to resign yourself to waiting until some researcher announces: "We have now discovered exactly how extrasensory perception operates. You now have permission to use your psychic senses." Even though science does not yet understand how psychic messages are processed, you *can* experience and use them in your daily life.

Scientifically Exploring ESP

From my early experiences I knew psychic ability was real. More than anything else, I wanted to find a way to help all people to develop their own ESP in a practical way. This was one of the main reasons for my attraction to brain science and biomedical chemistry courses at MIT. I wanted to learn what science knew about the brain, the mind, and the wiring of the nervous system. I hoped to find clues there for how to stimulate increased psychic sensitivity.

My favorite professor at MIT was Dr. Jerome Letvin, a mind-boggling, lovable eccentric. Imagine comedian Lou Costello with hippie-length, thinning gray hair, wearing baggy pants and beat-up old tennis shoes, and you have a picture of Professor Letvin in the 1960s.

Dr. Letvin was a pioneer in the study of exactly how nerve cells work. He constantly questioned what science knew and welcomed the challenges of the unknown. To this day I recall his opening words to our class in nerve study: "I am not going to teach what we know about nerves," he said. "Everything we know would take about two class sessions to tell you, and is relatively boring. Instead I am going to talk about what we *don't* know about nerves."

Dr. Letvin's approach changed my outlook on life: I began to seek answers from the unknown, not just the known. No longer would textbook science be my only avenue for exploring the extrasensory world. Personal experience and unorthodox investigation would provide equally valid avenues for me.

Like many others at the time, I was experimenting with biofeedback, the then-new method of affecting such automatic body functions as blood pressure and pulse rate with the conscious mind. We in the West were just learning what yogis in India had known for centuries: that the mind could control the autonomic nervous system, which regulates those functions. In Dr. Letvin's class I learned that the connections of the nervous system are so extensive that virtually any single nerve cell can "communicate" with any other nerve cell in the brain or body. The possible interconnections are literally unlimited. Exploring that concept, I tried a different biofeedback approach to lowering my pulse rate. Instead of merely thinking about being calm, I focused all my attention in my heart. Riding those unlimited nerve connections, I channeled my full awareness to my heart and pictured it slowing down. To my amazement I lowered my heart rate to 39 beats per minute. In previous weeks I had never been able to get it below 50, and that frequently took half an hour of meditating about calmness.

If I could achieve that result by focusing my attention on the location of my heartbeat, I wondered if my extrasensory skills could be improved through a similar form of locational focusing. During the next year I increasingly noticed that all my psychic impressions seemed to fall into four categories—those I felt, saw, heard, or just "knew" intuitively—and that with each type of extrasensory experience my attention was drawn to a different part of my body.

To pinpoint the location of greatest psychic sensitivity I practiced focusing on more and more precise areas of my body, and matched them to any increase or decrease in my psychic sensitivity. It was like playing a psychic game of "hot and cold." Each day I worked on a different psychic sense, learning to trigger that particular extrasensory channel in my dealings with people, and in the daily decisions I had to make. (The methods by which I learned to do this—and by which you will learn to do the same thing—will be explained in detail in the chapters that follow.)

The breakthrough was revolutionary, but basically simple. It involved two facets: (1) finding the precise focal points where extrasensory vibrations are received; and (2) realizing that we have four psychic senses rather than, as was commonly believed at the time, only one "sixth sense." For each of the four psychic senses there is a specific location on (or around) the body that serves as a natural antenna to pick up and amplify the psychic signals. I named these special places the "Psychic Reception Areas."

The Experiment That Proved the Theory

The key experiment that substantiated my theory that ESP could be tapped effectively via the Psychic Reception Areas occurred when I was working and studying one summer in the biology department at the California Institute of Technology (Cal Tech). A researcher in brain science was testing left-handed people for their ability to discern spatial relationships. Neurological findings suggested that the speech center in the brain of many left-handers spreads into both the right and left hemispheres of the brain (as opposed to right-handers, whose speech center seems to be in the left hemisphere only). The researcher reasoned that if this were true, the more crowded right hemisphere in left-handers must work less effectively at its other tasks.

The researcher focused on the right hemisphere's function of discerning spatial relationships. He set up a variety of experiments in which the subject had to feel various hidden curved shapes and decide which of several different-sized circles they came from. If the theory was correct, left-handers should do less well at the task than right-handers.

And they did. Right-handers were scoring 16 or 17 correct answers out of 20 tries; left-handers were scoring only 11 or 12 "hits."

As a left-hander, I realized this was a perfect opportunity for me to test my extrasensory skills and my theory of selective focusing. I got the researcher's permission to take his test—and use whatever sensing methods I chose in making my decisions. By focusing on the Psychic Reception Areas to help me identify the hidden shapes, I scored 19 out of 20 on the first test and 20 out of 20 on all the others. The experimenter, not surprisingly, was somewhat upset. I was accused of everything from cheating to being "the exception that proves the rule."

But of course I had not cheated. I had simply used my four psychic senses to extend my abilities. From then on the world of psychic perception opened to me steadily, and my once-limited ESP quickened and deepened.

Testing the Discovery with Others

Now I wanted to find out if the Psychic Reception Areas worked as well for others as they did for me. My first test subjects were fellow students at MIT, and members of the Boston-area psychic community. Marie, a leader in the latter group, was noted for the accuracy of her premonitions. She told me, however, that she occasionally had "blocked times" when she could not sense intuitive impressions for her clients. She would return their fee but feel badly that she was unable to help them. I respected Marie's sincerity. I knew all psychic readers experienced this same problem, and that the less honest ones would make up information.

I told Marie where the Intuition Psychic Reception Area was located, and taught her how to tap into it mentally. When I saw her again two weeks later she was brimming with renewed vitality and enthusiasm. She told me that three times during those past two weeks she had experienced psychic "blocks." In each case she focused on the Psychic Reception Area, as I had shown her, and each time intuitive impressions flooded into her mind. Two clients whose meetings with Marie coincided with her use of the Psychic Reception Area reported that those sessions produced the most accurate information they had ever received from her.

Testing my discoveries further, I found that use of the Psychic Reception Areas enhanced virtually everyone's psychic success. Most important, it proved equally effective with men and women who were not previously skilled in the psychic arena. For example, I met one evening with a group of people who had for some time been trying to see auras but unfortunately had not been at all successful. I shared with this group the location of the Vision Psychic Reception Area. Almost immediately all but one of them saw an aura for the first time.

Word of those successes with Marie and with the group brought me many eager volunteer test subjects. They, too, found that knowing the location of the Psychic Reception Areas opened up new psychic abilities for them, or enhanced abilities they already had. For example, Carol, a physical therapist, used the Feeling Psychic Reception Area to psychically "feel" which areas of her clients' bodies most needed massage and stretching exercises. Carol let her hands follow the feelings she was receiving and massaged the areas most needing stimulation. As a result she often was able to cut a client's recovery time in half. Moreover, clients who sometimes had felt drained by the sessions now said they felt energized by them. Carol's reputation with the physicians she worked for grew, and she was soon busier than ever, thanks to additional referrals.

Even the most practical of endeavors, I discovered, could benefit from a person's knowledge of the Psychic Reception Areas. For example, I recall a man named Ben, who owned a car dealership in a Boston suburb. He used the Hearing Psychic Reception Area to better listen to the engines of the used cars he bought as trade-ins. Ben also listened psychically as the owners talked about their cars. In one instance he heard in his mind the unmistakable sound of stripping gears—and got the owner to admit that the car had a history of recurrent transmission problems. Thanks to utilization of his Hearing Psychic Reception Area, Ben was taking fewer trade-in lemons!

For people new to ESP, the knowledge of Psychic Reception Areas increased their innate psychic ability to a level where they could recognize it and use it. Those who had already experienced ESP found that their speed, accuracy and control were enhanced. Since that time I have field-tested the Psychic Reception Areas in many parts of the world. During my voluntary service as a naval officer, I visited psychic groups in various countries and refined my methods to make them workable for people from all cultures and backgrounds. They can and will work for you, too.

An Introduction to the Four Psychic Senses

Psychic Feeling is most closely intertwined with our physical being. Its Psychic Reception Area is at the front of the body, extending from the top of the diaphragm to just below the navel. This area, often called the solar plexus, is the site of many nerve junctions. The extrasensory impressions received here are, quite literally, "gut" feelings. They are often accompanied by uneasy physical sensations ranging from vague discomfort to actual nausea or even abdominal pain.

Because she knew these symptoms can be a warning of imminent danger, a New York opera singer was able to recognize a message from her psychic feelings and use it in a desperate effort to save her husband's life. Stella had seldom worried about flying; after all, she routinely took commercial planes to make her appearances in the many far-flung opera houses. But after she married Paul, an international business-man who traveled mostly on smaller company jets, Stella panicked every time they flew together; every time he flew alone she felt even more uneasy and fearful.

After Paul rebuffed her entreaties to stop using small planes, Stella for years managed to keep her uneasiness to herself. One day her husband called to say he was leaving for Saudi Arabia in his client's small plane. Stella instantly felt a tightening in her abdomen. She found it hard to breathe, felt nauseated and experienced a total sense of panic in her gut. Associating those physical sensations with a warning psychic feeling, she called Paul back and begged him not to make the flight. She sounded so upset and was so insistent that he almost agreed to switch to a commercial flight. In the end, however, because Paul didn't believe in ESP, he told Stella she was just being overemotional. Paul learned too late the reality of Stella's psychic feelings. The commercial flight made it safely to Saudi Arabia but his small plane crashed in the desert with no survivors.

Psychic Intuition, or "knowing," is the most fleeting and evanescent of the four psychic senses. It is an inner aware-ness, unsupported by any particular internal sensation or external stimulus. You just know! The Psychic Reception Area for intuition is the crown and top of the head. Picture an open funnel extending upward from the center of the brain, widening as it emerges from the top of the head. That funnel is, in effect, a direct conducting pathway to the corpus callosum, the nerve bundle that links the two hemispheres of the brain. To tap Psychic Intuition you simply think upward and note your impression or intuitive knowing.

Most of us have occasionally "known" what another person was going to say before he or she spoke, or "knew" the outcome of a situation before the event itself took place. Dr.

Marlene Shiple, a Phoenix, Arizona, psychotherapist and a Free Soul instructor, tells of a more striking example of Psychic Intuition and how trusting it prevented disaster for her:

> I was driving 60 miles an hour along an undivided four-lane highway when I suddenly *knew* that the car on my right was going to pull into my lane and cut me off. There was nothing in the driver's actions to warn me: The car was in the middle of its own lane, moving smoothly; there was no turn signal flashing. Yet I knew what was going to happen.

Marlene hit her brakes at the same instant the other car veered into her lane. "If I hadn't," she says, "I would either have been hit or forced into a head-on collision with oncoming traffic to my left."

The reception areas for *Psychic Hearing* (sometimes called clairaudience) are on each side of the head, just above the ears. This is the area of the brain's temporal lobes, that section of the central nervous system closely associated with auditory processing. Psychic Hearing manifests itself as inner sound: Words, phrases, even paragraphs of inner dialogue may impress themselves on you as if through psychic stereo headphones.

Sometimes the clairaudient impression of a familiar song can even be meaningful. Consider the experience of a woman I know who had been divorced for three years and was ready for a new relationship but wondered if she would ever meet a special man again. While waiting on an open train platform one cold, blustery March day, Gloria heard a song being played: "I'll be with you in apple blossom time."

Gloria looked around. She was alone on the platform, far from a radio or any other source of music. Sensing that the song was in her mind, she asked herself a question: "When is apple blossom time?" and focused on hearing above ear level. Again her inner radio clicked on: "One day in May, I'll come your way . . . in apple blossom time."

Gloria forgot the incident until early May, when she visited a friend in the country and noticed that apple blossoms were flowering. Two days later she had a blind date and met the man she knew she had been waiting for.

To find the Psychic Reception Area for *Psychic Vision,* simply close your eyes. You will notice that with your eyes shut your visual awareness automatically shifts upward—it moves from eye level to the level of your forehead. This is the location the ancient philosophers used to call the "third eye." Open and close your eyes several times until you can be sure you sense that shift of attention.

There are two types of Psychic Vision. One is Aura Vision, which enables you to see the psychic energy field that surrounds each of us. When you observe and interpret another person's aura you are, in effect, taking a psychic X-ray of his or her personality, motives, and intentions. The second type I call Clairvoyant Image Reception, which registers visual psychic impressions directly on the mind's eye through pictures, images, or symbols. It is almost like watching an internal television screen.

Psychic Vision happens to be my greatest psychic strength (although everyone has all four psychic senses, each of us is stronger in one or two of them). One of my most striking experiences with Psychic Vision occurred some years ago when I was hoping to make my first lecture on ESP in Los Angeles. I was daydreaming and looking at my calendar when I suddenly saw the words *"Lecture in L.A."* appear in the empty space for Thursday, November 20.

I decided to follow my vision—but quickly ran into a stone wall. Every radio or television talk show I called in an effort to arrange some prelecture publicity either turned me down or was fully booked. Still, each time I looked at my calendar with Psychic Vision, the same image appeared in the November 20 space. So I went to Los Angeles anyway.

Once again I began my round of phone calls. This time a producer for one of the major television talk shows said, "We've just had a cancellation for tomorrow morning. We'd love to have you on, but it will only be for a few minutes." That was the good news; the bad news was that my search for a place to speak was proving more difficult. On such short notice I found only two available locations. One was centrally located and very reasonably priced but held only seventy-five people; the other was on the fringe of the city, expensive, and held two hundred people—that would be more than twice the response I had ever had from a television interview.

I thought, "I really need a sign for which meeting room to choose." Almost at once in my mind's eye I saw a billboard alongside a freeway. It bore the words *"ESP Lecture Here Tonight"* and an arrow pointing to the hotel with the larger room. I knew there was no such billboard in reality. Then I realized, "Of course! I asked for a sign, and that is exactly what I got!" With renewed confidence I turned the brief television interview into a major success, and my lecture audience filled the large room. By following my Psychic Vision I had been able to share with thousands on television the message of practical psychic sensitivity, as well as successfully conduct the first Free Soul training ever held in Los Angeles.

Know Your Psychic Strengths

Everyone can learn to focus on the Psychic Reception Areas in order to enhance *all* of his or her psychic abilities. But as you become more adept at the process you will find that one or two of your four psychic senses are dominant—easier and more reliable for you to use. This means you are discovering your natural psychic strengths. (The strengths of our physical senses vary in much the same way. For example, some people learn better when they can see or read a lesson; they are visual learners. Others learn more effectively by listening, and still others by using their sense of touch to get a "feel" for the task at hand. Teachers of early reading and writing skills are trained to spot these differences and to teach in a way that best meets each student's sensory needs.)

Those of you high in Psychic Vision we in Free Soul call *Visionaries.* Those who primarily feel their psychic impressions are called *Feelers.* Those whose strength lies in Psychic Hearing are *Audients.* Those who receive psychic impressions intuitively I call *Prophetics.*

Everyone has all four of the psychic senses, but for simplicity and efficiency it is important to know which psychic senses are your *best* channels for ESP.

A useful analogy is to think of the way one radio or television station always comes in best for you. It doesn't make sense to listen to or watch a fuzzier station when you have a clearer alternative. The same is true psychically. For example, it is ridiculous for people high in Psychic Feeling to waste time and energy trying to develop extensive clairvoyant skills while ignoring their clearer feeling channel; prophetic people will be less effective if they ignore their quick intuitive impressions while trying to receive louder psychic hearings.

Not understanding this concept of different psychic strengths is the biggest cause of slow psychic development. Trying to function psychically through your weaker ESP channels is like trying to swim upstream and can be highly frustrating. I frequently meet men and women who feel they are psychic failures because they cannot see an aura. Yet these same people invariably prove to be psychically strong in other areas.

Consider the example of Bill, an early student of mine in Tucson, Arizona. For nearly five years he had been trying to see auras and had been completely frustrated. To make matters worse, he had been studying with a group of people who were obviously high in Psychic Vision. They frequently saw auras and had vivid mental images in their meditations, while he was getting nothing. Bill was at the point of declaring himself psychically retarded and of giving up altogether.

When I pointed out that his aura indicated he had natural strengths in Psychic Feeling, Bill recalled how he had always received impressions about people as a feeling sensation without seeing their auras. He further remembered how in meditations, feelings flooded through him that frequently proved even more informative than the pictures fellow students described.

Bill felt as if the weight of years of trying to sense in the wrong way had been lifted from his shoulders. He left the class knowing that he was, in fact, psychic, and knowing how he could practice and improve his ability. Moreover, he decided that in his work as an employment counselor, he was going to stop trying to see psychically the job that was right for his clients; instead, from now on he would trust his inner feelings about which interviews to send them on.

When next I saw Bill several months later, he told me his placement percentage had doubled. For the first time in years he was truly enjoying his work. Additionally, his meditations were now relaxing experiences rather than tense tests for him. By following the inner feelings he received while meditating before work each day, Bill frequently anticipated opportunities. The most notable examples occurred when he felt and found job openings for his clients even before the jobs were announced.

Like Bill, once you learn your natural ESP strengths and use them properly, you too will be able to get the clearest and most accurate psychic information. Further, you will be receiving it in the manner that is best for you.

Discover Your Psychic Personality

As you read the following chapters on the individual psychic senses and hear the stories of my students and instructors, you will begin to identify and become familiar with your personal psychic strengths. You will also gain new insights into your psychic personality.

I have learned that the order in which you use your psychic senses directly affects how you live your life. For instance, if you are high in Psychic Intuition, you will automatically prefer to trust your inner knowings. If your strength lies in Psychic Vision, visualizing and reviewing all your options before making decisions is a way of life for you. Psychic Feelers love to feel the pulse of life but frequently feel overwhelmed by the impressions that bombard them; separating their own psychic feelings from those they pick up from others is essential. Those high in Psychic Hearing will naturally tend to talk to themselves and analyze the world around them through these inner conversations.

When you understand your psychic strengths and personality, each day becomes an adventure in self-knowledge and greater achievement. And when you understand the psychic personality of those around you, you can communicate and interact with them more easily, effectively, and lovingly. Here are some things to look for:

• Are there people in your life who refuse to plan ahead? Chances are they are not being irresponsible, but are psychically intuitive by nature and will know what to do when the time comes to do it. When they say "I know" before you have finished describing your thoughts, they are not being rude. They *do* know.

• Because Visionaries have an inner picture of the way things should be, they will not easily embrace a new idea. If you push them to make a snap decision, you will almost certainly get "no" for an answer. Give them time to work it into their picture and you will get a more positive result.

• Feelers need to feel comfortable about everything they do. It is almost painful for them to be in an environment that feels unpleasant. A touch or a hug is as important to them as the business at hand.

• Audient people are the direct antithesis of Feeling people. Because they operate from an inner hearing and understanding, they tend to tune out feelings. As a result, they are analytical, assertive, even harsh. You may mistakenly think they dislike you because Audients seldom realize how strongly they are affecting others.

This is just a taste of some of the insights into life that you can gain once you see the world from a psychic perspective. Each of the next four chapters on the individual psychic senses will help you not only to develop that particular form of ESP, but will also make clear the reasons behind many of your personality traits and your reactions to those around you.

• 2 •

Psychic Feeling—The Body as a Psychic Antenna

OF THE FOUR psychic senses, Psychic Feeling is the most accessible. It is the easiest to open and to interpret. Surely there were times when you sensed a dangerous situation before the danger became apparent? Surely there were mornings when you woke feeling something wonderful would happen to you that day, and it did? All those inner sensations you probably thought of as "gut feelings" or "instincts" are in fact psychic impressions, plucked from the energy field that surrounds us.

All people, places and objects constantly radiate vibrational patterns, and your physical body is like a large antenna able to register and assimilate their meaning as inner feelings: *I feel there will be problems with this project. . . . Everything feels just fine. . . . I have a feeling something's wrong in the baby's room.* (there's hardly a mother who hasn't sensed *that* warning signal, acted on it, and arrived just in time to prevent an accident).

Sue Leonard, a Free Soul instructor in Evergreen, Colorado, had just such an experience. Camping in the Rockies with her husband and two young children, Sue readied her baby daughter, Lisa, for bed while her husband and son collected wood for the evening's fire. When Lisa wouldn't settle down in her small sleeping bag, Sue got the baby's car seat, in which she invariably fell sound asleep, propped it up in the tent, and strapped Lisa in.

After dinner Sue's sense of peacefulness in the mountain twilight was suddenly jarred. She felt as if she were choking. "I knew instantly it was Lisa," Sue recalls. "I ran to the tent and found the baby had twisted in the car seat so that its straps had gotten wrapped around her throat, making it impossible for her to breathe or cry out. Lisa's face was turning blue." Sue frantically untangled the straps just as the baby was about to lose consciousness. "She started to breathe again, her color returned. I knew that my Psychic Feeling had saved my baby's life."

If you are naturally gifted in Psychic Feeling, your personality profile will read something like this:

- Primarily, you are concerned for and about other people.
- You can usually sense when something is troubling others, and are ready to give of yourself freely to help.
- You trust your feelings implicitly.
- You are relatively unconcerned about time and deadlines.
- You make every effort to put others at their emotional ease and expect them to be equally caring about your feelings.

At the same time, however, Psychic Feelers must protect themselves against the vibrational onslaught of psychic pollution in their environment. Many of your negative feelings—tension, depression, anxiety—are actually not yours at all;

they are other people's feelings that you are picking up. In most instances, once you understand what is happening you will quickly be released from the effects of those psychic disturbances.

Another Free Soul instructor, Dr. Fran Mandell, tells of a client who moved to Manhattan from a small town: "For five years in New York City, Jill went from doctor to doctor, seeking help for her fatigue, anxiety, and feelings of unexplained anger. All of her physical tests were normal. As a naturopathic physician, I thought she might be suffering from a food allergy. But that proved a false trail, too."

Oddly, Jill said she felt better when she stayed at home, indoors; the symptoms returned only when she went out. "I began to sense that Jill was high in Psychic Feeling," says Fran, "and that walking the crowded Manhattan streets was exposing her to the exhaustion, anxiety, and anger vibrations of hundreds of strangers." After Jill learned to understand and control her sensitivity to Psychic Feeling, she was able to live as healthily in Manhattan as she had before she moved there. "The psychic sensitivity Jill didn't know she had had been working against her, rather than for her," says Dr. Mandell. "She had assumed all the negative feelings that overwhelmed her were her own."

The Feeling Psychic Reception Area

Psychic Feeling is the one extrasensory channel that is most often linked to a physical sensation. Sue actually felt as if she were strangling; Jill actually experienced the physical symptoms of tension and anger. Although your entire body can function as a Psychic Feeling antenna (that's why you can sense someone sneaking up behind you), the focal point lies in the abdomen from the top of the diaphragm to just below the navel—specifically, the solar plexus. What you feel

Figure #1   The Feeling Psychic Reception Area

can be as mild as "butterflies" or as strong as a knot in the pit of your stomach.

That the solar plexus functions as a "master antenna" for Psychic Feeling should not be surprising. Numerous nerve networks associated with the autonomic (or involuntary) nervous system are located there, spreading over the abdomen like a latticework of fine wires. The autonomic nervous system not only provides direct access for psychic impressions to the subconscious mind, but it also is linked to every major organ and most endocrine glands. As such, it maintains and regulates all of the body's vital automatic functions—pulse, blood pressure, fluid balances, respiration, metabolism, and so on—and is viewed even in medicine as a natural monitoring mechanism.

Moreover, the metaphysics of Eastern beliefs hold that the area of the solar plexus is the energy center—or *chakra*—most closely linked with creativity and emotions. It is thought to be where the spiritual and physical worlds join. Little wonder, then, that the solar plexus is a key reception area for psychic energy patterns.

Whichever explanation you find more acceptable, the result is the same: You can use the sensitivity of this region as the focal point for fine-tuning Psychic Feeling. You can tap it as your Feeling Psychic Reception Area.

Extensive testing at MIT confirmed this for me. In one of my experiments I tried to identify the color of different colored cloths by "feel" alone, with my eyes closed. I held the cloths on different parts of my body. I received the strongest impressions and the most correct results when I held the cloths over my abdomen. In another experiment I moved my hand toward the body of test subjects whose eyes were closed. Most people were able to "feel" the presence of my hand at a greater distance from their body when I held it at the level of their abdomen; if my hand was at the level of their face or chest I had to move it much closer before they could sense its approach.

You may not have realized it, but you demonstrate the psychic sensitivity of this abdominal region almost intuitively every day. Have you ever noticed that you turn your body to face objects or people when you want to sense them more deeply? Think about your body language when you feel uncomfortable. Don't you cross your arms in front of that solar plexus area to feel more protected and less vulnerable? Of course you do. The extra mass of the arms helps to buffer the Psychic Feeling bombardment. Turning sideways or sitting behind a desk can provide similar protection.

Accessing Your Feeling Psychic Reception Area

You are about to have your first "on command" experience with Psychic Feeling, using it to tap the vibrational energy around you. As you focus on your solar plexus and practice the steps outlined below, remember that you are sensing for a *feeling*—not a picture, or a word, or an intuition. Also keep in mind that the sensations you receive at first will usually be subtle rather than intense.

A few suggestions before you begin:

- Learn to ask yourself what you are feeling. Do not accept "nothing" as the answer.
- If you think you feel nothing, ask yourself "What kind of 'nothing' is this?" Is it "nothing" as in "nothing different"? "Nothing" in the sense of a void or vacuum? "Nothing" in the sense that something is missing, or being hidden from you? Sometimes the "nothing" you sense may actually carry a great deal of information.
- If what you feel comes to you as "feeling good" or "feeling bad," ask yourself: "In what way good? Why do I feel bad? Where are these feelings coming from? Is it a fleeting feeling, or something more permanent?" Continue until you can discover more precisely what you are sensing.
- In the early stages of practicing this exercise, keep your eyes closed. It's quite possible to psychically "feel" with your eyes open, but I recommend closed eyes in the early learning stages to cut down external distractions.

Start·by sensing the energy of your current location:

1. Relax your body by taking several deep breaths and slowly exhaling.

2. Sit or stand comfortably, facing away from anyone who is present, and close your eyes.

3. Focus your awareness on the solar plexus area and feel the impressions you are receiving.

4. *Don't try.* Don't force. Just be open and aware. You should feel as if you have full access to the master antenna in your solar plexus area.

5. Note the impressions you experience. Does the room feel calm or vibrant? Does its energy feel sluggish, smooth, or scattered?

6. Briefly go to several other rooms or environments and tune in the same way. Compare any differences in feeling you sense from each location.

Sensing People with Psychic Feeling

Now let's practice tapping your Psychic Feeling a bit more by thinking about several people you know, one at a time. Note the sensations you experience in your abdominal antenna as you mentally focus on each person. How do they feel to you? Loving and kind? Angry or frustrated? Do they make you feel sad? I believe you will find some difference, some uniqueness of feeling about each individual. When you sense psychically this way you are using your feeling ESP to identify and remember the aura or vibration of the people you are thinking about. This type of practice will help you develop the skilll of psychically feeling people "on command." As a result, you will rarely be fooled by anyone's words or behavior. You will feel just what to expect.

Sensing people who are physically present is as easy as

sensing the aura of those you simply bring to mind. Remember to stand or sit facing them to allow your Psychic Reception Area to receive the person's total output of vibrational energy. Gently but steadily identify the feeling sensations you receive in your solar plexus area. I try to get an initial Psychic Feeling impression each time I shake someone's hand. I continue to sense them more in depth as we speak. (Don't be obvious about your actions, however; people may get a bit nervous if they realize what you are doing.)

Try this exercise at work, at home, or in a social situation. See if you can sense how best to approach your boss or a co-worker. See if you can feel what happened to a friend earlier in the day. Try to grasp the mood of a family member, sense what may be on his or her mind.

Trust Those Subtle Feelings

The key to success with Psychic Feeling is learning to accept and interpret even the most fleeting or subtle impressions. Ali Habib, an international businessman in Washington, D.C., and a graduate of Free Soul training, recently recalled how he used Psychic Feeling to help him hire a key assistant from among three equally qualified and competent women candidates.

"Usually I can make a quick decision in such matters," he said. "This time I was puzzled. I had no way to choose among them except via my psychic impressions." Where Patricia was concerned, Ali vaguely sensed a future event that would alter her suitability for the position. With the second woman, Anne, everything felt positive until she mentioned her husband. At that moment his sense of Anne seemed to vanish. She referred to the man several times in the course of the interview, and each time it felt as if Anne were no longer in the room. With Cheryl, the third candidate, his psychic feelings were the most positive, the most comfortable.

Ali hired Cheryl, trusting his feelings about the other two women. As things turned out, he made the right choice: "Patricia won a law school scholarship a few weeks after the interview and moved to Boston. Anne also moved away when her husband was transferred to the West Coast by his employer. Cheryl went on to become one of my best staff members."

Psychometry: Psychic Feeling Through Your Hands

Even though the solar plexus is the main Feeling Psychic Reception Area, your hands can be used to make more direct contact with what you want to feel. Psychic vibrations travel from your hands through the body to the abdomen, where they are magnified. This technique is called psychometry, and you can experience it in either of two ways:

1. Hold an object in your hand and note the impressions you receive in your solar plexus. Does the object make you feel good? In what way good? Do you feel sad? Why sad? Keep sensing until you are satisfied you have felt all the vibrational impressions of the object.

A friend's ring or an old one you have in a jewelry box is a good object to begin with because metal retains vibrational energy. Sense your feelings about the ring and the person who has been wearing it. Is it a new ring, or an antique? If it is antique, is the wearer the original owner or are you sensing a prior owner? Share your impressions with the owner of the ring. Most likely your impressions will prove surprisingly right.

2. Run your hands over an object or down a list of items and note the feelings produced in your Feeling Psychic Reception Area as you touch or pass each item. You can practice this type of psychometry the next time you buy something. Whether you are trying to decide which of several similar items will last longest, or you just want to select the ripest cantaloupe in the bin, you can scan with your hand and sense with your solar plexus.

The Hands as Scanning Sensors

This second form of psychometry served me well some years ago when I was a naval officer stationed in Italy on the U.S. Sixth Fleet flagship. As a newly promoted lieutenant, junior grade, I was given the job of monitoring the ship's maintenance. The Navy at the time was particularly concerned about the high number of mechanical breakdowns caused by improper maintenance, and fleetwide inspections were frequent. The inspectors were a particularly unsympathetic lot. To set an example for others, they seemed intent on finding ways to fail a ship.

The new Navy maintenance procedures were exacting. The slightest deviation from the prescribed steps would be reason for a black mark. I was caught between perfectionistic inspectors on the one hand, and, on the other, salty old chief petty officers who had been doing maintenance work *their* way for years—on irregular schedules, using whatever grease or oil was at hand rather than making an extra trip to get the exact lubricant the rules specified. Each department claimed its maintenance record was flawless. I knew otherwise, but I had to prove it.

I resolved to use my psychic abilities to help prevent disaster. I carried out my own mini-inspection, using Psychic Feeling to sense for incomplete or incorrect maintenance. I ran my hand down the written list of the scheduled tasks, noting the sensations received in my solar plexus area. Scanning via this hand-feeling connection, I sensed which jobs had been poorly done, and which had not been done at all. Those were the ones I asked to inspect. As a result, close to 75 percent of my spot-checking showed problems. This gave the appearance that had the ship been inspected right then, it would have failed abysmally.

When I reported my findings to my captain, he was furious. I still remember the look on the faces of the officers and chiefs when they were called on the carpet by him to explain. He ordered a total reemphasis on correct maintenance procedures, and when the inspectors arrived we were ready for them. They searched and probed but could find virtually nothing wrong. Our ship got a 94 percent rating, highest in the Atlantic Fleet that year and the crew was rewarded with extra time ashore. On a personal note, I won early advancement to the rank of full lieutenant—and believed even more in the practical value of psychic sensitivity.

Are You a Psychic Feeler?

Now that you have had some experience testing your Psychic Feeling, see if you can discover the degree to which you rely on that aspect of psychic sensitivity. A "yes" answer to four out of five of the following questions suggests that you are high in Psychic Feeling. After you finish this quiz we'll explore why and how the questions—and your responses—are significant indicators of Psychic Feeling sensitivity:

1. When you enter a room are your first thoughts about how the room feels to you? Do you think, "I feel comfortable [or uncomfortable] here"? (__Yes __No)

2. How do you form your first impression when you meet a new person? Does a feeling about him or her strike you first, or do you respond to how the person looks or sounds? Do you think, "I feel comfortable with this person; I sense he or she could be a good friend"? (＿Yes ＿No)

3. If faced with potential danger, do you feel it before you think about it? Do you often feel uneasy? (＿Yes ＿No)

4. When you must make a decision, is your first priority a need to feel comfortable with the solution, rather than automatically choosing the most logical course or visualizing all the possibilities? (＿Yes ＿No)

5. When buying new clothes or furniture, do you choose items you feel comfortable with, or do you follow the latest fashion or trend? (＿Yes ＿No)

Question 1—How do you sense your environment?

There are many ways to sense a room *psychically* when you first enter it.

- A person high in Psychic Vision is likely to see auric colors or shapes.
- The clairaudient individual may hear thoughts or fragments of conversations that took place there.
- Anyone high in intuition will just "know" what happened in the room.
- Those high in Psychic Feeling sense the vibrations in the room as feelings.

Recall the time you entered a room where an argument just took place, and you felt tension in the air? You were using Psychic Feeling to sense the remaining patterns of the intense energy produced by the quarrel. If a happy event had occurred in the room you would have felt its lighter-hearted vibrations.

Not surprisingly, the "feel" of the environments in which you live and work are important to you if you are high in Psychic Feeling. If there is any residue of negative feelings, you will notice it immediately and not feel comfortable until the vibration is changed. Here is a graphic example:

Rachel, a New York psychotherapist, spent many months searching for the perfect living space—a place intimate and festive enough for the parties she loved to give, yet calm and spacious enough for the serious work of the therapy groups she conducted. She finally found space in an abandoned Greenwich Village factory that was being converted into loft condominiums.

There were two drawbacks, however. Rachel had to buy the space sight unseen from a floor plan, since the factory was being gutted. And it would take six months before the reconstruction work was finished. Rachel was so delighted with her find that she signed the purchase papers anyway.

The six months extended to twelve before Rachel could move in. "The job was delayed by constant arguments among the workmen," the builder told her. But the night she moved in Rachel was so pleased to be in her new home that nothing mattered. Exhausted from the chores of moving, she fell into bed. But sleep would not come. Nor would it come easily for many other nights, for Rachel felt extremely uncomfortable in the loft. No matter how cheerily she decorated it, her sense of disquiet grew.

Then Rachel learned that the arguments that had taken place on her floor had been so violent that several of the workmen involved in them had been seriously injured. Suddenly Rachel, a gifted Psychic Feeler, understood the source of her negative sensations. And she knew that if they could not be banished she would not be able to stay.

Her solution was just what a Psychic Feeler would think of—she gave a weekend-long party for all her friends. For forty-eight hours the loft was filled with music, dancing, eating, drinking, laughter, and good conversation. Several Free Soul graduates who attended commented, "There isn't a negative vibration here that can survive this party!" And none did. Rachel has been happy there ever since.

Question 2—When meeting new people, how do you form your first impressions?

If you are high in Psychic Feeling you would first sense the other person's energy field to see if it feels comfortable to you. What you are actually but subconsciously doing is sensing the other person's aura. Dr. Fran Mandell, who as we learned earlier is strong in Psychic Feeling, has a unique method for sensing a male friend before she goes on a date with him. She scatters some brain-teasing games on the coffee table before he arrives, and suggests he try them as she prepares some light refreshments. While he works on the games Fran senses his vibrations.

"The point," she explains, "is that while he is working on the puzzles he is not focused on me. Often a new man projects the kind of feelings he *wants* you to pick up; this way, he is projecting an aura that is more accurate, more honest. Having an accurate feel for how a date will treat you may take some of the fun of discovery away, Fran says, "but it does help you communicate better, and in some cases it can put you on your guard against an overly assertive or controlling partner."

Question 3—When faced with potential danger, do you feel it before you think about it? Do you often feel uneasy, or have "butterflies" in your stomach?

To a Psychic Feeler, discomfort in the solar plexus area (queasiness, perhaps even pain) is a warning of impending danger. The sensation can be likened to an internal radar system that alerts you to the approach of a physically threatening situation. Consider the case of Karen, one of my early Free Soul students.

An attractive, friendly, and trusting young woman, Karen had experienced little in the way of psychic sensitivity when she met a particularly pleasant young man at a party. She was drawn to him in many ways—but the closer she came to him physically the more apprehensive she felt. The tightness she felt in her solar plexus seemed to be telling her to get away from this man before he overpowered or assaulted her.

Instead of making a firm date with the man that night,

Karen took his phone number and promised to call him the following week. She left the party confused and annoyed with herself—she could not quite understand why she had let someone who seemed to be so right just slip through her fingers. But a few evenings later she understood quite clearly, when she saw the man on the evening television news. He had been arrested on a charge of raping a woman he had met at the same party.

Question 4—When faced with having to make a decision, is your first priority to feel comfortable with the solution rather than picking the most logical answer, or visualizing all the possibilities?

The first priority for persons high in Psychic Feeling is to feel at ease with their actions and responses. To Feelers a decision is logical only if it feels right. It may not be the kind of reasoning others are accustomed to, but it makes sense to Feelers. When people high in Psychic Feeling actively stay attuned to their feeling antennae, the results can directly improve their decisions. In some cases it can even save lives. Luce Neyra, a critical-care nurse and one of Free Soul's instructors in Virginia, worked in the high-risk maternity unit of a local hospital. Her job demanded strict attention to any sign of trouble that might affect a pregnant woman or a newborn child.

"This particular night," Luce recalls, "a high percentage of our patients were women whose pregnancies had been difficult, or whose earlier deliveries had been risky ones." Having been trained in Psychic Feeling, Luce was using her body antenna to sense for any problems as she made her rounds. She often found she was alerted to trouble long before physical symptoms of the problem developed. Moreover, she had refined a method of "feeling" into the hospital rooms as she walked by them. More than once she had sensed something that made her check out a patient earlier than she normally would.

"Of all the women due to give birth this night," says Luce,

"we expected the least trouble with the woman in Room 119. But as I passed her room an overwhelming feeling of urgency flooded through me. The doorway of the room seemed to be pulling me in, like a powerful but invisible vacuum."

Luce entered the room, went directly to the fetal monitor and saw unmistakable signs of the baby's distress. She summoned a doctor at once. He found that the umbilical cord had been wrapped around the baby's neck, cutting off the flow of oxygen. Quickly he turned the baby and freed the cord. The delivery that followed was quick and normal. But if Luce had not acted on her Psychic Feeling the infant might well have been stillborn, or brain-damaged.

Luce is not alone in trusting her ESP as a day-to-day part of her nursing decision-making. An article in the January 1987 issue of *The American Journal of Nursing*, called "How Expert Nurses Use Intuition," provides many other examples of how critical-care nurses tap more than their physical senses in caring for patients' needs.

Question 5—When buying new clothing or furniture for your home, do you choose articles you feel comfortable with rather than trendy items?

The Psychic Feeler will wear comfortable clothes. This does not mean he or she ignores style. Feeling comfortable about how one looks is important, but not as important as wearing clothes that feel comfortable. Where a Visionary might not be able to pass up a pair of shoes that are just the right color, the Feeler won't even consider buying them if the heels are too high, or if they pinch a bit. If you visit a Feeler's home you can always expect a comfortable chair to sit in and thick carpets to wriggle you toes in. Feelers will decorate with soothing colors. And usually you'll find a cuddly pet to nestle in your lap.

Mary Kendzierski, a Feeler and Free Soul instructor, is a senior member of our headquarters staff. She has an associate degree in interior design and is continuing her education in art and arts management. Although her educational background makes her quite aware of style and color, as a Feeler she dresses first for comfort. There is not a tight waistband, binding shoulder, pinching shoe, or stiff fabric in her wardrobe.

Mary's home similarly reflects her need for "feeling" comfort. Soft, nonglaring lights and comfortable chairs provide the relaxed atmosphere she likes to live in. When she is studying or doing work at home, you will usually find her surrounded by large pillows on her bed rather than sitting rigidly at her desk.

How to Relate to a Feeler

Whether or not you scored high on Psychic Feeling, you have to relate to Psychic Feelers in your daily life. If you are in a close relationship with one of these subtly sensing individuals, you may find that their feelings are easily hurt. After twenty years of psychic research I have learned a great deal about the different psychic personalities and would like to share a few insights about how best to relate to Psychic Feelers no matter what your own psychic strengths may be.

• Not only are the feelings of Psychic Feelers easily hurt, but they will always be concerned about how *you* are feeling. If the day's pressures make you tense and irritated, Feelers will pick up those vibrations and assume you are upset or angry with them. Tell them that is not the case, and let them know the real reason you are upset. In return you probably will get the best comforting and caring you have received in a long time. (You might even get a great back rub as a bonus!) If you have a problem and really need assistance, Feelers will come to your aid. Giving them the opportunity to truly feel needed is the greatest kindness you can share with them.

• Because Feelers are so sensitive, they easily pick up your negativity and magnify it. Go out or get away from their immediate area when you want to be angry. Forcing them to be around you when you are radiating unpleasant feelings is as painful for them as being angry at them personally. The same is true when you are in an intense and rushed work mode. Feelers will be uncomfortable in this kind of environment. Those of you who are not as strong in Psychic Feeling may not even notice the intensity of the vibration you are radiating. Feelers are not weak or wimpy; they literally *feel* the tension ten times stronger than you do.

• When you are upset with a Feeler personally, even a brief outburst can cut the person like a knife. Yet Feelers forgive as readily as they are hurt. As easily as they receive unpleasant feelings, they soak up and absorb feelings of apology and love. Always let them know you love them even if you don't like what they did. Also, no one more appreciates being cared about when he or she is hurt than a Feeler.

Feelers Have Their Own Style and Sense of Time

They truly run on a different clock from the rest of the world. Because a feeling takes longer to interpret and process than a thought or picture, Feelers can seem to be working in slow motion. Those of you who are more naturally intuitive or psychically visual may grow impatient with the feeling person. Remember that time and deadlines are always less important to them than how they feel. Pressure doesn't work on them. It just causes them to feel worse and slow down even more. The best thing you can do with Feelers is let them work in their own space at their own pace.

Don't force them to be rigidly logical, either. If you are a highly logical or mental person, the Feeler may seem like an irrational, emotional nightmare to you. Remember that they think with their feelings. No matter how well-thought-out your plan may be, it's no good if it *feels* wrong to them. For Feelers, trusting their feelings *is* the most logical approach. You won't budge them until you present a version of the plan they can feel comfortable with.

The Secret to Success with Feelers and Psychic Feeling

As you step out into your world, see if you can tell who the Feelers are. With all you have learned in this chapter, I hope you know the type of behavior to expect of them, and see them for the caring, highly sensitive people they are.

Best of all, you will be able to join them in the world of sensitivity. Because you know the Feeling Psychic Reception Area, you can tune in "on command" to Psychic Feeling when you want to tap this form of ESP. You will quickly be able to improve many areas of your life—for example, by hiring the right employees as Ali did; by sensing when others need assistance, as Sue and Luce were able to; and by avoiding dangerous situations, as Karen did.

Practice using your own Psychic Feeling to sense those around you who seem high in Psychic Feeling. They will project strong signals for you to discern and interpret. Feel for the best way to greet them and put them at ease. Practice sensing when they need a hug or a sign of your support. The successful psychic results you receive will bolster your confidence and accelerate the development of your own Psychic Feeling abilities. Never ever pass up an opportunity for that feeling embrace. Whether it is a sincere handshake or a full-fledged Feeler hug, it will energize you psychically and physically.

The Gift of Psychic Feeling

ADVANTAGES

Most natural of the psychic senses
Easiest of the psychic senses to develop
Best psychic sense for discerning and interpreting subtle
energy patterns
Best psychic sense for empathizing with others
Best psychic sense for monitoring safety and personal protec-
tion

DISADVANTAGES

Psychic sense that most easily picks up others' negativity
Hardest psychic sense to turn off or shut out
Psychic sense that makes it hard to remain detached

People High in Psychic Feeling

STRENGTHS

Are the most sensitive to the feelings of others
Keep life and work feeling comfortable and livable
Give of themselves sincerely and are "people" people
Are flexible and best at adapting to keep everyone happy
Trust their feelings and can "feel" when something is not
right
Are best at sensing subtle signals
Are the best huggers

WEAKNESSES/THINGS TO BE AWARE OF

Are prone to pick up other people's feelings, good or bad
Are prone to being psychically overloaded
Can become overemotional or easily overwhelmed by feelings
Can have trouble being on time or meeting deadlines
Are very susceptible to being hurt by rejection

• 3 •

Psychic Intuition—The Gift of Prophetic Knowing

"AND IT SHALL come to pass in those days . . ." was the phrase with which the Old Testament prophets began their predictions of future events. They spoke with certainty, but not because their forecasts were based on logical reasoning or on statistical evidence. The Biblical prophets simply *knew*—and from knowing, they prophesied.

In its own way, Psychic Intuition, of all the psychic senses, most resembles the kind of instantaneous knowing that for millennia has been the hallmark of prophecy. People high in Psychic Intuition often seem to have that same gift. I call these men and women Prophetics.

Are you one of these intuitive people? If so, you probably feel that the rest of the world is functioning in slow motion. Your mind works quickly. You experience flashes of unexpected insight. You leap ahead to certainties no one around you is yet aware of. During a conversation with a friend you probably say "I know" long before your friend has finished telling you a piece of news or sharing a feeling. You may even sense much of what we are going to be talking about in this chapter. You may at this very moment be saying to yourself, "I knew he was going to say that!"

This chapter will help you become aware of how to make the most of your Psychic Intuition. You will learn to understand the characteristics of the intuitive personality. No longer will you wonder why you always seem to be finishing other people's sentences. You will experience what it is like to refine your Psychic Intuition, and learn to tap intuitive information without questioning how or why you know it. And you will be given enough evidence of the validity of Psychic Intuition so that you will come eventually to put full trust in your own prophetic knowings. Moreover, you will discover how using your Psychic Intuition can make your life calmer, safer, more successful, and put you more in tune with the universe.

Jacquie is an example of someone high in Psychic Intuition—one of those persons who always seem to be at the right place at the right time. Jacquie's day beings at 7 A.M., when she awakes in time to turn off the alarm clock *before* it begins to buzz. "I knew it was just about to go off," Jacquie will say if you ask her how she manages that trick.

Jacquie hails a taxi and gets in. On the way she has a sudden intuition that there is a traffic jam ahead. Acting decisively on her "hunch," she pays the driver, leaves the cab, and takes the subway for the rest of the trip. Jacquie arrives at her office precisely on time for her morning's work. By profession Jacquie is a trend forecaster; she predicts what people will be doing, wanting, buying in the near-term future. Today she is dressed for business in the latest Georgio Armani suit and top-of-the-line Avia jogging shoes. If she pays any attention at all to those who glance at her unconventional outfit, she enjoys their perplexed expressions.

She brushes aside a pile of phone message slips, closes her

office door, seats herself comfortably, and meditates for ten minutes. Meditation completed, Jacquie calmly returns those phone messages she knows are important, files the rest for future attention, quickly skims the essential items in *The New York Times, The Wall Street Journal, Women's Wear Daily,* an assortment of European and Japanese magazines, and the morning's Doonesbury comic strip. All the while she is freshening her makeup.

Jacquie's first client is the head of a food brokerage company. The firm is planning its product line for the next five years. The owner, a warm but meticulous man, wants her views about food-buying trends in the years ahead. Intuitively, Jacquie knows that although he is friendly, the executive is subtly testing to see how knowledgeable she is about his field. Jacquie tells him of the growing popularity of fish-substitute products such as imitation crabmeat made from a fish called pollock. She alerts him to a new line of foods made from poultry that is processed to taste exactly like beef. She shows him a new, more economical way to package food items; she has designed it herself.

Jacquie's presentation is exciting, imaginative, and comprehensive. Her client is impressed and pleased. He overlooks the somewhat chaotic condition of her office—which would ordinarily turn him off—gives her a check as a retainer, and tells her to draft a consulting contract for the coming year. As he leaves he notices Jacquie's jogging shoes and smiles, knowing he is dealing with a unique individual.

Jacquie typifies the Psychic Intuitive. She is unconventional, up on all the latest trends, an innovator, and she has a seemingly limitless fund of creativity. In short, she is in constant knowing touch with all parts of her world.

I am sure you know people like Jacquie: They are the idea people in your life, the ones you call to find out the "in" place to eat, to shop, or to vacation. They are quick-minded, the first to laugh at a joke or complete a crossword puzzle. They are flexible, ready to try anything new and exciting at a moment's notice. Although they can easily anticipate problems, you will not find them worrying. They know intuitively what the solution will be.

Not Just the Future

The association of Psychic Intuition with prophecy has led to the wrong idea that this form of extrasensory perception can be *only* about the future. Psychic Intuition *is* the most future-oriented of the four psychic senses. But any one of the four can be utilized for premonition or prediction: A precognitive impression can come in the form of a vision of the future, a feeling of warning, or even a psychic hearing. Why, then, is Psychic Intuition so strongly associated with premonition in people's minds? There are two reasons.

The first reason is that all too often we tend to talk ourselves out of other types of precognition. Visual and feeling premonitions frequently are downplayed, mistakenly being labeled imagination or "inner fears." Precognitive hearings also are easily passed off as "talking to oneself."

The second reason is that because psychic intuitions arrive out of the blue, often with no supporting evidence, they catch our attention. When the intuition or psychic impression does in fact prove true, one more readily remembers having had the precognition. The result is that the vast majority of premonitions we actually acknowledge *do* come through Psychic Intuition. As a result, Psychic Intuition is commonly called Prophecy and mistakenly linked only to future sensing.

Psychic Intuition is ESP that occurs not as a vision, a voice, or a feeling, but as an instantaneous knowing. That knowing can be about the past, the present, *or* the future. Each type has its own benefits. Let's examine all three.

In the Present: The Intuitive Psychic Telegram

Both Dena and her daughter Sheila are high in Psychic Intuition. There has always seemed to be a "knowing connection" between them. That Sheila was born on Dena's birthday seemed to bring them psychically even closer. Once when Sheila was working as a television production executive, she was flying back to New York from Miami when an engine on the wing of her plane exploded and burst into flames. Sheila, whose seat was on that side, could see the fire eating along the wing edge. The plane started to lose altitude rapidly. Food trays, parcels, and luggage ricocheted around the cabin as the plane bucked out of control. Some of the terrified passengers were hysterically shouting, "We're going to die!" But Sheila remained calm: She just knew that everything would be all right. Her Psychic Intuition told her not to worry. And her intuition proved correct. The pilot regained control, shut off fuel flow to the burning engine, and used his remaining power to limp to an emergency landing on a foam-covered runway at Langley Air Force Base in Virginia. No one was seriously injured.

Once safely inside the base officers' club with the other passengers, Sheila's first thought was, "I've got to let my folks know I'm okay." Her efforts to phone them were fruitless, however, as they had already left for New York's Kennedy Airport, where Sheila was scheduled to land, to pick her up. Unable to make phone contact, Sheila repeatedly sent the thought to her mother that she was safe. Meanwhile, officials of the airline at Kennedy were telling those awaiting the plane's arrival that it was lost. Dena remembers that even at the moment, she sensed a calming message and "knew" there was no need to worry. Suddenly she said, "I've got to call Langley Air Force Base." "What on earth for?" Sheila's father asked. "I just know that Sheila is there," Dena replied.

Dena had never before heard of the Langley base and didn't even know where it was. Fortunately, the telephone operator did. You can imagine the look on everyone's face in the officers' lounge at Langley when a security guard asked for Sheila and said, "Your mother is on the phone." Sheila and Dena exchanged the amazing details of what had happened to each of them. Then Dena returned to tell the others anxiously waiting for loved ones that the plane had landed safely and no one was seriously hurt. The airline was mystified; Sheila and Dena were not.

Dena and Sheila's story is an example of using intuition to psychically "know" what is happening right now. It is prophecy in the present tense. Although they may not be as dramatic as Dena's, surely you, too, have had experiences with this type of Psychic Intuition. For instance, the times you just *knew* you had to call someone. Or the times you berated yourself for not following a hunch that turned out to be right. Now you can understand that those flashes and hunches were your Psychic Intuition at work. Remember, you can trust them to help make your life easier.

Psychic Intuition Solves a Mystery from the Past

That same type of instant intuitive insight can also solve mysteries from your past. Science tells us that every light ray is still shining somewhere; so too, then, must every psychic vibration still echo far out in the cosmos. With Psychic Intuition you can tune in to those vibrations from the past, frequently with life-changing results, as the following story illustrates.

Angela, a shy, naturally attractive young woman, was one of my Free Soul students in Colorado. Though I saw her only once a week, it would have been difficult not to notice that she was trying to hide her good looks. I wondered why she grew embarrassed or even angry if anyone complimented her on her appearance. But it was not until our third session—when we practice a technique that examines how one has been trained to feel and act about one's appearance—that I discovered why Angela downplayed her loveliness. The technique requires that you examine the attitudes and values your family members had about personal appearance when you were growing up, and write them down in a notebook. I saw that Angela was distressed by this assignment. She fidgeted in her seat, had trouble writing, and averted her eyes from those around her. Suddenly she burst into tears. When she calmed down a bit, she told her story to the group.

Angela had been raised by a much older sister, Barbara, when their mother died early in Angela's childhood. "My sister always made me feel guilty about how I looked," Angela said. "Whenever I wore bright, attractive clothes she criticized me and made me take them off. All I could ever wear were 'plain Jane' clothes, never anything eye-catching or sexy. It was the same with makeup. Barbara never let me use any. And every time my father would compliment me, my sister forbade me to wear that outfit again."

Angela said she could not understand why her sister wanted her to look dowdy: "Barbara was attractive; she took pride in her own appearance. Why did she try so hard to keep me from looking feminine and pretty?" During her teen years Angela alternated between hating her sister and feeling some inexplicable guilt.

As Angela grew older the sense of confusion about her appearance affected her relationships with men. Though outwardly pretty, inwardly she felt unattractive and withdrawn. Her feelings of inadequacy prevented her from enjoying her femininity, and from responding to a man's romantic interest. Knowing that Angela was high in Psychic Intuition, I suggested that she try to sense back psychically in time.

Perhaps it would help to identify the cause of her sister's strange behavior if Angela were to receive key intuitive insights. "Don't focus on yourself," I said. "Rather, scan for some event in your sister's life."

Angela did what I suggested. She began by meditating, by gradually letting her thoughts go back in time and scanning her sister's childhood. To her amazement, an impression jumped out at her. Angela suddenly and intuitively knew that as a girl, Barbara had been sexually abused by their father. Hard as it was for Angela to talk to her sister about this psychic impression, she knew it was vital for them to discuss it. Barbara was first stunned, then angry, and then, caught completely off-guard, she allowed the years-long barriers of silence to fall away. Twenty years of bottled-up emotion poured out as Barbara recounted her hidden shame.

The incident had taken place before Angela was born. "I was only thirteen," Barbara said. "One night before going to bed I tried putting on some of Mother's cosmetics—powder, lipstick, rouge. Then I decided to try on one of Mother's nightgowns." At that point her father came into the room and made a sexual advance toward her. Although the situation stopped short of actual intercourse, Barbara always felt ashamed of what had happened and blamed herself for it. Barbara never told anyone of the incident. She herself carried the double burden of shame and guilt. Somehow those feelings got twisted into an obsession—that she must keep Angela from the same fate by making her look unattractive. Barbara never realized how much her behavior hurt her sister until they were able to talk honestly together about it. Afterward the two women were able to heal the wounds that years of misunderstanding had created.

When I saw Angela next she was a changed woman. Her hair was cut and styled to highlight her beautiful face. She comfortably wore a sensual knit dress that, though conservative, radiated allure and her pride in her femininity. In short, by using her Psychic Intuition to probe the past, Angela had changed her life—and probably her future as well.

Are there mysteries from your own past that still need to be brought to light and resolved? What unexplained matters have you wanted to know more about? Try using your Psychic Intuition to see what flashes of insight may come to you. Do this by bringing back to mind that unexplained or enigmatic event and slowly reviewing it. Try to see it in a mental picture, or try to recall your feelings about it. As you do, note whatever immediate impressions or thoughts come to you about this unresolved area or question. Do not try to analyze those impressions or thoughts immediately. Just make a note of them as they occur to you. Later, review your notes and see how they explain or illuminate those areas that were previously unclear to you.

Although Psychic Intuition occurs rapidly, these "out-of-the-blue" insights contain a great deal of information. And once you learn how to use the Intuition Psychic Reception Area (see pages 62–64) you will be able to trigger those first impressions and insights even more easily. The fact is that when you receive a psychic knowing, you are actually acquiring a great amount of data that has been condensed into an instant awareness.. When you learn to trust this intuitive information, you can benefit in many ways, whether dealing with the present, sorting out the past, or scanning the future.

Psychic Intuition and Future Events

Simon is a Wall Street stock analyst and one of the financial community's best-known mutual fund advisors. One day in September 1987 Simon and his friend Ruth met for lunch at a quiet Italian restaurant on the east side of Manhattan. Somewhere between the antipasto and the cappuccino,

Simon told Ruth he expected the stock market to go into a severe tailspin in the near future. "Sell everything," he counseled her.

Ruth knew Simon had been accurate before in his sense of future trends, so even though the market itself was reaching new highs every day, she followed his advice. When friends—who, not having been warned, lost large amounts of money in the crash that occurred that October—asked Ruth how she had made such a seemingly illogical decision, she said: "I just knew Simon was right."

Later, Ruth asked Simon how he came to be privy to information that no one else seemed aware of. "There was no specific information, no specific data," he replied. "If I had reacted just as a market analyst, I would have said, like my colleagues, that the market was still headed upward. But I had a 'knowing'—it was so strong I could not ignore it." Simon was so certain his Psychic Intuition was telling him the truth that he closed out all his client accounts and his own account before that "Black Monday." Not one of his clients lost a penny.

Wouldn't you like to have a Prophetic like Simon as your financial advisor? The truth is that you don't need a Simon in your life. All you need is to know where your own Psychic Reception Area for prophecy is located, and how to use it to tap your Psychic Intuition at will.

The Intuition Psychic Reception Area

The Psychic Reception Area for prophecy is located at the top of the head. To access your Psychic Intuition successfully, direct your thought and attention upward. It's as simple as that. *Just think "up."* Picture a funnel shape opening its larger end through the top of your head and extending outward toward the universe. To intuitively evaluate a person,

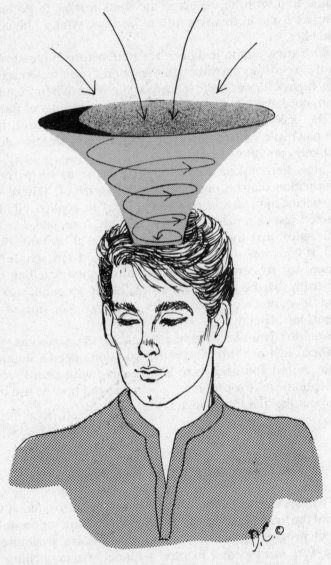

Figure #2   The Intuition Psychic Reception Area

place, or future happening via psychic knowing, focus your awareness upward and note your intuitive first impression. (We will show you exactly how to do this in the material that follows.)

The neurobiological basis for locating the Intuition Psychic Reception Area at the top of the head is that the central fissure of the brain lies there. That central fissure provides the most direct and unobstructed pathway to the corpus callosum, the massive nerve bundle that interconnects the two hemispheres of the brain. With the recent emphasis on the advantage of using both the right and left sides of the brain, access to their primary connection may well be of profound importance. Moreover, shifting your awareness upward to the crown of the head consistently causes a marked increase in alpha-brain-wave activity—the brain-wave pattern most frequently associated with altered states of consciousness and increased extrasensory ability.

Metaphysically, the region of the aura that surrounds the top of the head has traditionally been viewed as an opening to higher states of consciousness. Many Eastern philosophies believe this area to be the location of the crown chakra, the access point to greater spirituality, and suggest focusing one's awareness there to enhance the power of meditation.

Whatever explanation you accept, the fact remains that you no longer have to wait for a psychic impression to strike you in order to be intuitive. By tapping this Psychic Reception Area, you can open this sensitive channel any time you need or want additional insight. You can prophetically compare your future options or decisions. You can quickly scan a person's potential, or monitor the status of current events and locations. You have the ability to be intuitive "on command." Furthermore, you have a specific method for practicing Psychic Intuition, and you can refine the accuracy, depth, and clarity of your impressions.

Tapping the Gateway to Psychic Intuition

Let's try tapping your Intuition Psychic Reception Area. Follow the simple steps below for your initial experience with your channel for unlimited psychic knowing:

1. Relax, sit comfortably, and close your eyes.

2. Picture a funnel, its *wide end* extending up and out from the center of the top of your head.

3. Gently guide your awareness upward and focus your attention out through that funnel. Be open to whatever you experience.

4. Remember, do not try too hard; do not force your concentration!

5. Practice alternating between your normal eyes-open awareness, and thinking up with your eyes closed (turning your attention upward to the Intuition Psychic Reception Area).

6. Feel how a multitude of impressions seems to be pouring into your mind through the funnel. Notice the sensation of heightened attunement that opens to you there.

Did that seem too easy? Well, there is nothing that says being psychic has to be hard. Actually, Psychic Intuition is the easiest of the ESP channels to switch on once you know how. That upward-thinking process, almost literally, opens a door to universal knowledge so that instant information can flow in. For example, a pregnant Washington, D.C., graduate of Free Soul used the process and was rewarded with knowledge of the exact time of her daughter's birth and the child's birth weight, three weeks before the baby was delivered. In another instance, a student told me that Psychic Intuition allowed him to know the answers to test questions for which he was unprepared.

I used a similar version of this upward-thinking process to

improve my academic standing at MIT. Being new to ESP at the time, and with my skills in that area not yet fully developed, I took a different approach. I tapped my Intuition Psychic Reception Area *before* studying for exams so that I could sense ahead of time what subject areas would be specifically covered by the test. Then I worked hard studying those particular sections. Using this technique helped me to graduate in the top ten percent of my class—even though as an incoming freshman I had been in the bottom ten percent of entrance exam scores!

Anyone can tap Psychic Intuition to help them with their daily information needs. The secret lies in knowing where and how to look.

I have demonstrated this technique to many professional psychics—men and women who have been using their natural prophetic abilities for years. When they learn about the Psychic Reception Area and how to access it they are amazed at how easy it is for them to trigger their intuition at will. Many say they felt that upward-focus shift when their "knowings" arrived, but they did not realize they could initiate the process themselves. Marie, the Boston psychic who used my methods to help break through her "blocked" times, is just one example of this phenomenon. Crystal, a professional psychic for ten years, provides another.

Crystal had a problem with a client who spoke so slowly, who took so much time to pose her questions, and who digressed so much while asking them, that the psychic felt that her own impressions and spontaneity of response were being distorted by the delays. Once Crystal learned about the Intuition Psychic Reception Area she simply waited until the client's rambling stopped before shifting her awareness upward and receiving her first psychic impressions.

The key to intuitive knowing is to capture your psychic impression the instant you open that psychic door. By learning about the Psychic Reception Area Crystal discovered how she could control the timing of the door's opening.

Intuition is the fastest of the four psychic senses. Sometimes it is hard to grasp and hold on to your psychic intuitions because they are so fleeting—they arrive quickly and then vanish just as quickly. Indeed, you can easily miss them entirely if you hesitate to accept them or fail to focus rapidly. The key is to capture your *first* impression. If you ignore it, or wait for a slower, stronger or more lasting awareness, you will miss these psychic lightning bolts entirely. (Write them down as they occur and go back over your notes later for verification.)

This quickness does have its advantages, however. Psychic Intuition is the best form of ESP to use when you have to tune in rapidly to a number of separate places. By shifting up to your Intuition Psychic Reception Area and bringing each location to mind, you can sense many remote areas in a short time. One of my most memorable experiences with this technique came when, as a naval officer, I used remote sensing to motivate my men.

Remote Sensing via Psychic Intuition

As an ensign, one of my first assignments was to supervise a division of fifty bosun's mates, deck crewmen who tend the ship's lines, paint its sides, load cargo, and run the shuttle boats that ply between ship and shore. Originally the bosun was the true seaman. In this modern naval age of radar and computers, this kind of deck duty is now one of the least desirable jobs aboard ship. Sailors assigned as bosun's mates are usually either those who fail to qualify for a technical post, or those who, having run afoul of the law, are given the choice of prison or military service. Their not-so-affectionate nickname among Navy personnel is "the deck apes." Being on the lowest rung of the Navy's professional caste system, my crewmen's morale was understandably low. Before I arrived on the scene they had in many ways been treated little better than slave labor. Their attitude and performance reflected that abuse. Prophetically, I knew they had the potential for excellence. My goal was to restore their sense of pride and self-respect while at the same time increasing their work performance. I knew I could achieve those results. I had already used my Psychic Intuition to scan the possible futures of my new assignment, and I sensed the high possibility of both group and individual success.

Sitting in my quarters, I shifted my focus upward and tapped my Psychic Intuition again. This time I let my creativity flow. Soon I envisioned a plan to turn those possibilities into realities. I assigned each man to a work area based on his preferences, and laid out a schedule of tasks for the week. By giving each seaman his own area of responsibility I hoped to inspire in him a sense of self-worth, to provide a way for him to show initiative. I also told the men that when the work was satisfactorily completed, they would be given free time. If a job took until Saturday to finish, the men would have to work the extra day. If they finished on Thursday, they would have Friday off.

My plan was met with total skepticism and derision. I realized that the men's cynicism was understandable, based on their past experience with casual mistreatment. In the past, when they finished a task early they were just given another unpleasant work assignment. They only way I could prove I would keep my word was to ensure that each man *did* finish early—no small task with this bunch!

Since the forty-plus work locations were spread all over the ship, it was impossible to physically check each work crew with any regularity. To meet that challenge I used Psychic Intuition. With it I was able, via remote sensing, to keep track of what was going on at each of the different work areas. I sat in my quarters and psychically scanned each area periodically. As I brought each location to mind I would tap my Intuition Psychic Reception Area and note my immediate impression. In scanning, I searched particularly for those areas that were falling behind schedule. When I located one I went directly to it. My crew could never understand how I always seemed to show up just when they started goofing off.

The result? I kept the entire division working at maximum efficiency. Everyone finished his job by Thursday, and everyone was rewarded with the promised day off. I repeated the procedure the next week. After two weeks of working efficiently enough to get Friday off, the men knew that the deal I had offered was real. From then on the system took care of itself. My crewmen were commended for professionalism and self-motivation. The men spent less time in trouble and more time enjoying liberty. I won an early promotion and was given executive opportunities exceeding my rank. And all these accomplishments were due to the practical use of Psychic Intuition.

Experience Your Remote Sensing Ability

You, too, can use your Psychic Intuition to tune in to any location at any time. Choose a location, hold it in mind, and note your first impression. It's as easy as following the simple keys below:

1. First, select a remote location you wish to scan.
2. Next, determine what it is you want to sense about it. Is someone there? What is happening? Are your instructions being carried out?
3. Then, with your eyes closed, hold each location in mind.
4. Shift your attention upward to your Intuition Psychic Reception Area. Note your first impression and write it down.
5. Follow up by calling or going to the location you sensed to see how accurate your impressions were.

You can use this brief process to "check in" psychically whenever and wherever you wish. Try it now with several locations for practice. The instant information you receive can help you avert problems, make better decisions, be at the right place at the right time. Because it is so quick and simple, remote sensing through Psychic Intuition can be an important time-saver for busy people.

New Approaches Through Psychic Intuition

People present the most complex challenges we deal with daily. Each individual is unique and sometimes difficult to understand. How you deal with others is often the key to success or the cause of failure. Psychic Intuition can help by giving you new and more creative insights to apply to interpersonal relationships. You may be surprised at how these insights can improve your understanding of and communication with other people—especially those with whom you have business or personal problems. The insightfulness of Psychic Intuition provides information and answers that are otherwise unavailable. Because Psychic Intuition is that unlimited open funnel to the universe, it can tap a wealth of creative methods and approaches.

Bringing Hope to a "Hopeless" Case

Dr. Marlene Shiple, a Phoenix, Arizona, psychotherapist and Free Soul instructor, uses her Psychic Intuition in her work to sense for new information and new counseling approaches that can better help her patients. Early in her career Marlene was a therapist in the chemical dependency center of a Houston, Texas, hospital. Brad, a patient in his late twenties, was fast becoming one of the drug rehabilitation unit's biggest failures. Fancying himself a James Dean in cowboy boots, Brad was mad at the world. He had been placed in the CDC by the joint decision of his parents and his wife after drug abuse almost destroyed his life and theirs, but he resisted all efforts to help him.

With only a week left in the twenty-eight-day program before he was due to be discharged, Brad showed no improvement at all. He was chronically late for group therapy sessions. When he did arrive he acted bored, or frequently tuned out the group altogether. His individual counseling sessions with Marlene proved equally fruitless: Usually they just gave Brad an opening to rage against everything in his life. They ended with his still unshaken belief that nothing was wrong with him.

One day, while thinking about Brad's case, Marlene intuitively sensed that it was the right time to go to his room and talk with him. She found Jan, another member of the counseling team, already there, and on the receiving end of Brad's abusive bombast. Because it was hospital policy that only one counselor at a time work with a patient, Marlene started to leave. Suddenly she knew she should stay. Intuitively, Marlene knew something had to be done to shock Brad into a realistic view of his life. An idea suddenly occurred to her. She caught Jan's attention, and Jan indicated with a nod she would follow Marlene's lead. (The two therapists had recently discussed the value of intuitive ideas in counseling situations, so Jan was eager to see what Marlene now had in mind.) Marlene began to talk to Jan as if Brad were not present. Gradually she steered the conversation to Brad's lack of progress, talking openly about what they felt his prognosis would be once he was released. Still speaking to each other as if they were alone, they described in detail how Brad's young daughter would surely grow to hate him; how he would soon be living on the streets after his family gave up on him; and how prison was probably in his future. Brad fell silent for the first time since he arrived at the CDC. Now he was listening—and listening hard.

At no time in her training had Marlene heard of this therapeutic approach. Speaking negatively in the presence of a patient was strongly condemned and strictly against policy. Yet, Marlene intuitively knew the approach would work, and Brad's silence told her they were getting through. For several more minutes the two counselors continued to word-paint the worst possible picture. Finally Marlene said what a shame it would be for Brad to end that way, because both she and Jan agreed that the coming tragedy could so easily be prevented. Still paying no attention to Brad's presence, they left the room.

Brad's behavior began to change dramatically. He spoke up sensibly in group therapy sessions and even asked to have a joint counseling session with his parents. The turnaround was so remarkable that the hospital extended Brad's stay, and when he left the hospital he was well on the way to a successful recovery. When Marlene last heard from Brad, he was reconciled with his parents and living happily with his wife and daughter, had remained drug-free, and had a steady job as an apprentice carpenter. By following her Psychic Intuition—even in the face of therapeutic convention and hospital policy—Marlene found a successful way to reach Brad.

Intuitive Insight into the Problem People in Your Life

You can use your Psychic Intuition, just as Marlene did, to gain insight into the best ways to deal with difficult people in your life. Which individuals seem always to misconnect with you? Which are stubborn? Uncooperative? Aloof?

Wouldn't you like to know how to relate and communicate with them better? In today's increasingly stressful world, anything that helps you get along more smoothly is a blessing. Using Psychic Intuition to tune in to others is a gift you can give yourself. Not only does it lead to greater success, but it also can directly improve the quality of your day. Learn to trust your intuitive instincts. Try using the following method:

1. Think of three people with whom you have difficulty (boss, in-law, neighbor).

2. One at a time, hold each person in your mind and focus on ways to improve your relationship with him or her.

3. Shift your attention upward to your Intuition Psychic Reception Area and note your impressions.

4. Be open to any thoughts about what style or method of approach you might use. See also if you receive any intuitions about why these people react to you as they do (so you won't have to take their behavior personally).

5. Jot down your impressions and implement them the next chance you get.

Taking Charge of Your Life with Prophetic Psychic Intuition

The future is the hardest thing to sense psychically because it contains a virtual infinity of possibilities and probabilities. Because Psychic Intuition is the fastest and most unlimited of the psychic senses, it can condense those possibilities and probabilities into a clear "knowing." Instead of having slowly to compare myriad feelings, you can use your prophetic skills to compile an instant summary. This is what makes Psychic Intuition the best ESP channel for scanning the future.

You can tap your Psychic Intuition to review upcoming situations, decisions, or actions. You can intuitively notice when changes are needed or a matter is becoming urgent. You can also identify problems that will work out on their own without needing much of your attention. Simply check in with your Intuition Psychic Reception Area as you review your options. That takes only a moment, but it often can save you hours of debilitating worry. Here are the keys for this psychic future scanning:

- Bring to mind an upcoming decision you must make or problem you need to resolve.
- Make a brief list of your possible options (act now; get outside help; leave things alone; wait, but get ready to move quickly; and so on).
- One at a time, review each option in your mind.
- As you do, shift your attention upward to the Intuition Psychic Reception Area. Sense for which option intuitively seems the right choice.
- Jot down the impressions you receive for future action.

In effect, knowing how to use your Psychic Intuition is like having access to your very own crystal ball. It is inside your head. All you need to do is shift upward and tap it. Knowing your Intuition Psychic Reception Area, and being open to sensing without bias—not blocking out what you may not want to hear—is all that's required. This is an important point: Don't be afraid of sensing something not to your liking. Remember, *the future is always in motion and you can change it by your actions.* Your Psychic Intuition tells you only what the current trends are. If they are not moving in your favor, take action to bring about the necessary changes. In fact, use your Psychic Intuition to sense the quickest, easiest, and most effective ways to make those changes. This is what I call being in charge of your own destiny.

Prophetics Are the Best at Not Worrying

People high in Psychic Intuition naturally use their ESP to sense ahead. As a result they flow with life more freely. They have often experienced how decisions and solutions to problems just seem to come to them. Prophetics are the absolute best at not wasting energy on needless worry. They intuitively know when things will work out.

Consider the case of Julie and Ray, who were among the people at a weekend seminar I was conducting in Tucson, Arizona. We had just completed the exercise for sensing a remote location. Julie, naturally strong in Psychic Intuition, radiates the spontaneity it gives her; she is quick-minded but stays relaxed and easygoing. Ray, a retired Army officer, is naturally strong in Psychic Vision, with a talent for precision and organization. In many ways they are exact opposites. The impressions the couple received in remote sensing appeared to be similarly incompatible.

Both chose to sense their home, where they had left their teenaged children in charge while they were away. Ray, high in Psychic Vision, pictured the house when he tuned in. He saw a mess: clothes scattered all over, dishes unwashed—all the trademarks of youngsters on their own. "I knew we shouldn't have left them," he groaned. Julie, in contrast, tuned in to her Psychic Intuition and knew without a doubt that everything was and would be fine.

The couple's impressions were so at variance they decided to call home to see who was closer to the facts. As it turned out, both were right. "The house is a mess," their son said, "but we're just about to clean it all up. We'll be finished by the time you get home." Julie beamed: "I knew it would all work out!" She exemplifies the unwritten creed of intuitive people: "Why worry about what I know will work out anyway?"

Spotting the Characteristics of Different Psychic Personalities

This is just one example of how the Prophetic's approach to life is affected by his or her particular ESP strength. Of the psychic personality types, Prophetics are probably the easiest to spot. Their quick minds and the way they trust their intuition are giveaways. See if you can spot the Prophetic way of doing things in the following life situations and what psychic strengths lend themselves to the other options. Note also which choice sounds most like the approach you would take. What does that tell you about your psychic personality?

1. *Your present job has ended. To find a new job and further your career you—*
A. . . . systematically buy every paper and analyze every ad, deciding which are the most logical ones to apply for.
B. . . . picture yourself in several different jobs, and then search for the one that fits your mental pictures.
C. . . . answer only the want ads that instantly strike you and feel confident that the right job will come along.
D. . . . choose a job because you felt comfortable with the people you met when you were interviewed.
Prophetics "know" that the perfect work situation will come along. They would begin the job search by answering ads that seem to "grab" them. Their natural intuitive ability would put them in the right place at the right time. By the way, Prophetics do extremely well in job interviews. Since they intuitively know the needs of others, it is relatively easy for them to convince the interviewer they are the right person for the job. I am sure you already know that the Prophetic answer to the question is C. The approach described in A is how Audients would seek a new job, for they are logical and systematic. The Visionary would want to see

the picture (B); and of course the Feeler would need to feel comfortable (D).

USING PSYCHIC INTUITION TO ENHANCE YOUR VALUE AT WORK

Eddy Cettina, a Free Soul instructor in Los Angeles, is a striking example of how this Prophetic job-hunting style can lead to professional advancement. Eddy is an intelligent woman and a hard worker, but her strongest asset is her ability intuitively to anticipate her employer's needs. When the breakup of her marriage left Eddy with a mortgage to pay and a young daughter to raise, the "help wanted" ads became required reading. One ad seemed to jump off the page at her: She just knew she had to apply for the accounts-payable position a development and construction firm had listed, even though it was not the kind of work she wanted.

Although Eddy felt a sense of instant rapport with the president of the company who interviewed her, she at first turned down his offer of employment. She told him the salary wouldn't cover the bills she had been left with; more important, she explained that she felt her skills went beyond accounts-payable work. He then offered her a higher salary and asked her to reconsider. Eddy couldn't think of one good, logical reason to take the job—save for the fact that her intuition told her to go for it. As she had recently started a Free Soul class in psychic development, Eddy was aware that Psychic Intuition was her strength, and she trusted its value to her. Further, she felt she could "know" what the boss wanted without being told and that it would help her advance in the company.

Her boss signed all accounts-payable checks personally. Tapping her Psychic Intuition, Eddy was quickly able to prepare the ledger cards and files exactly as her employer wanted them. She also "knew" he would be pleased if she put together a job-cost breakdown, so she initiated the creation of those reports as well. By the end of the year Eddy was promoted to the post of administrative assistant. When she handled her boss's correspondence, Eddy would shift upward, tap her Psychic Intuition, and sense just how to write his replies. When business grew hectic she took on a variety of projects without having to bother her boss for instructions. He was so pleased with her work, and with the seemingly uncanny way Eddy anticipated his needs, that he promoted her to office manager for the entire firm.

His trust in and reliance on Eddy continued to grow. She used her Psychic Intuition to help him select new sites for development projects and as a result was promoted to vice president. Eddy's salary has more than tripled. Instead of lying awake at night worrying about how to pay the mortgage, she now owns rental property, has bought a home for her parents, and relishes the responsibility of the work she enjoys. Eddy's practical application of her Psychic Intuition has improved the quality of her life.

2. *You are single and have reached a time of life when you no longer want to be alone. To go about choosing a new partner you—*

A. . . . make a mental list of all the qualities you want in a partner, then set out to find someone who fits your list.

B. . . . are less concerned about the person's qualities, or how he or she looks, and care more about how you feel when you are with him or her.

C. . . . first form a mental picture of what your partner should look like.

D. . . . go by instinct, knowing you will be led to the right person at the right time.

Remember that Psychic Intuition helps Prophetics automatically to be in the right place at the right time. That characteristic is such a part of their lives that they trust Mr. or Ms. Right will show up if they follow their instinct. Since Prophetics are quick-minded, they will know without a doubt when the person and the moment are right. Therefore, the Prophetic's answer is D. Audients are the list-makers; given a choice they will seek a mate in a logical and organized way (A). Visionaries first notice how something or someone looks, so their image of the person would be very important (C). And Feelers, as we have noted before, always want to feel comfortable with their partners (B).

USING INTUITION TO FIND A LOST LOVE

Nothing represents being at the right place at the right time more than finding one's special love. Marianne Stanley, a Tucson, Arizona, Free Soul instructor and founder of an organization she calls "Friend Finders," used her intuitive abilities to find her own lost love. Marianne, a vibrant and warm woman, was separated from her first real love, Don, when her assignment in the Air Force and his in the Navy took them to different parts of the U.S. Marianne let their relationship drift until she eventually lost all contact with Don; it was a slipping away she regretted for more than twenty years. During that time both she and Don married other people and raised families. But she never forgot her first love.

Over the years Marianne heard, via mutual acquaintances, that Don was married and still in the military, but no one knew how to reach him. Then, twenty-three years after their parting, Marianne "knew" that Don would be coming back into her life. She didn't know how or when. She just knew she would be seeing him again.

Soon after that flash of intuition Marianne founded Friend Finders. She was so sure about getting in touch with Don again that she wanted to help other people locate their long-lost friends and loved ones. She mentioned her personal search during radio, TV, and newspaper interviews promoting Friend Finders, secretly hoping that some listener would know where Don was. Instead, Marianne's Psychic Intuition provided the key to putting her at the right place at the right time. That July her family was having its annual reunion in her hometown of Dayton, Ohio. Marianne had not planned to attend, but somehow suddenly she knew she had to: There came to her a compelling inner knowing. She had experienced it too often not to trust it.

The closer Marianne got to Dayton, the stronger her thoughts of Don became. She "knew" he must have returned there—and in fact he had done so after retiring from the Navy. She found Don's phone number—but then was temporarily stymied by old insecurities and fears of rejection. "Will he remember me? Will he still care about me? Will I just make a fool of myself?" she wondered. Then Marianne's intuition flashed again. She knew this was the perfect time to get back in touch. The impression conquered her fears. She called and once again found that her Psychic Intuition had served her well. Don's marriage had ended. His children were grown and on their own. As they spoke Don, too, knew that the moment for their reunion was at hand.

The happy ending to this story took place last December when he and Marianne were married. After twenty-three years a missed opportunity had been recaptured, and a lost love found because Marianne had successfully followed a psychic trail.

3. *In order to find a new place to live, you—*
A. . . . interview several real estate brokers, find the most competent one, and then review every home listed in your price range.
B. . . . find a broker with whom you feel comfortable and trust him or her to locate the ideal home for you.
C. . . . drive around the neighborhood you'd like to live in, find houses that look good to you, and ask to see those.
D. . . . simply know that the right place for you will turn up if you stay open and aware.
By this time I am sure you know which psychic skill is

linked to each answer. Let's try a self-test. Identify the answers in your head, then check them out at the end of this chapter. The logical, organized Audient would choose —; the Visionary planner who wants to see everything first would choose —; and the Feeler who always has to be comfortable would choose —. That leaves the Prophetic, who has learned to trust being in the right place at the right time. He or she knows the perfect situation will come along, and so chooses —.

Whenever my wife and I need to find a new home, Debbie's acute Psychic Intuition serves us well. She has a special ability to locate the perfect place for us to live. My first experience with Debbie's house-hunting intuition came soon after we were married and living in Italy while I completed my military service. During my bachelor years overseas I lived aboard ship, and so knew nothing about how to find a home in a foreign country. Debbie, after only a few days in Italy, walked into the housing office, checked the listings quickly, and, sight unseen, picked the one that was to become our home for two years. It turned out to be a two-bedroom, two-bath penthouse with terraces on three sides and ocean views on two. At a rent of only $175 a month, it was unbelievable luxury for a young couple.

When we returned to the U.S. we used both of our psychic strengths to find a home. As a Visionary I had used maps and clairvoyance to identify which part of the country would be best for us (Sedona and Oak Creek Canyon, Arizona). Debbie's intuition located what was to be our home for seven years.

When we arrived in Arizona, I, like a typical Visionary, drove around looking at everything within the circles I had drawn on the maps. Debbie, bored with my plodding Visionary ways, suggested we go down one specific forest road that intuitively felt right to her. Sure enough, she spotted a small, nearly obscured sign on the side of the road: "Unusual houses for rent or lease." I had missed it completely and would have driven right past it. What we found was the entrance to a group of rustic mountain cabins, hand-built out of natural stone and huge pine beams, nestled alongside beautiful Oak Creek and surrounded by a variety of forest vegetation. The location was perfect. The beauty was unparalleled. Best of all, the rent was almost half what we had expected. Are you surprised to know that the cabins were located precisely where two map circles intersected? Following our psychic sensitivity had served us well. (Later, when we had to move again, Debbie was guided to another house that was not yet even for sale. We now live in that three-level redwood house with a view for miles both up and down Oak Creek Canyon.)

Here is a final question that can give you another insight into the Prophetic personality.

4. *It is vacation time. You choose to go—*
A. . . . to an isolated spa on the Florida coast where you will enjoy the mud baths, massages, and warm sunshine.
B. . . . on a working windjammer cruise, spending a week as part of the crew, manning the lines, trimming the sails, and keeping night watches.
C. . . . traveling in Europe, visiting as many of its major cities as you can in your two-week trip.
D. . . . on a photographic tour of the Grand Canyon and other nearby scenic wonders.

A true Prophetic will choose a C-type vacation. Prophetics want to know, see, and do everything. They don't like to stay in one place for long; their minds work so quickly they need to keep moving to avoid getting bored. A Prophetic tourist will not leave a city before he or she has discovered all the "in" places favored by the local folks.

Traveling with a Prophetic is exciting, but it can also be exhausting if you are not of a like mind. I can say that from personal experience, growing up with my Prophetic mother, Aurora. When she came to visit me in Europe I knew the Continent was in for a whirlwind tour. True to her Prophetic characteristics, Aurora had intuitively known how to gather the best pretrip information and bargain tickets.

Buying a Eurailpass, for example (which for one low fare gives you three months of first-class train travel throughout most of western Europe and unlimited passage on some ships and buses), was a typical Prophetic's delight for Aurora because it allowed her total freedom to follow her intuitive decisions. With no time schedule to follow and no rigid itinerary, Aurora was at liberty to change her plans, deviate from her route, stay longer in one place than originally intended—and still catch the next train to wherever she wanted to go.

Most people who hear about Aurora's European travels think she spent years there; they can't believe anyone could do so much in so short a time. And everywhere she went Aurora let her psychic intuition guide her. Aurora was so competent at this psychic city-hopping that she even intuitively intercepted the train my wife and I were on in Switzerland. We were taking a brief trip to Berne, the home city of my wife's family, and had arranged to meet Aurora in Geneva. We had no idea that our letter, telling her the time of our arrival and where we would be staying, failed to reach her. So you can imagine our surprise when, at an obscure train station in the middle of Switzerland, Aurora walked into our compartment and sat down as if she had been expected at that point all along. Debbie was amazed, and I—well, I had grown up with Aurora, so I was used to seeing this quintessential Prophetic successfully follow her "knowings" through life.

How might other psychically sensitive people answer the question about vacation preferences? To begin with, Feelers would enjoy being pampered at a spa. Their primary need is to feel emotionally at ease, but physical pleasures also rank high on their list. Audients are the hard workers. Relaxation isn't real for them unless it also involves some kind of work or accomplishment. What could make a better "working" vacation than the challenge of mastering the seas in a sailing ship? They would return home from a windjammer cruise completely refreshed. Finally, Visionaries are the quintessential photographers, wanting to capture all the eye can see whether through the lens of a camera or by recording the sights in their mind's eye. A scenic trip usually rates high in their vacation choices.

If you understand these different characteristics of the various psychic personalities, you can plan family vacations that meet everyone's needs, or at least better understand the reasons behind each person's preferences.

Understanding the Prophetics in Your Life

Psychic Intuition is the most frequently encountered psychic strength. Of all four ESP types—feeling, seeing, hearing, and knowing—people high in knowing (the Prophetics) are the most numerous. You are bound to meet and interact with many of them. Getting to understand the quality of their minds, and learning how best to coexist with them, can add immeasurably to the quality of your life. Here is what you should know about them:

Men and women high in Psychic Intuition function at an accelerated pace. Since knowing is the fastest of the ESP channels, they operate in high gear all the time. Because Prophetics have natural intuitive openness, thoughts constantly flood into their mind. That can be distracting when you are trying to talk with them, or when you are pursuing a train of thought and they go off on an unrelated tangent.

But Prophetics cannot help having ideas pop into their mind. Nor can they "save" the thought for later discussion. Like psychic intuitions, the idea will vanish in an instant. They have to talk about it right away. One solution for dealing with this quality of the Prophetic character is to note the thought that's thrown out at you and file it—literally on a notepad or figuratively in your head—for future reference. If you give the Prophetics around you this kind of freedom to continue their mental zigzagging you will find yourself tapping a useful reservoir of intuitive insights.

Incidentally, many Prophetics believe they cannot meditate effectively because they find it hard to quiet their mind. They should not try to still that free flow of ideas, which is their natural strength. Instead, the key to meditation for a Prophetic is to allow the flow to continue, but to try to put it to one side while keeping a focus on the meditative thought.

Prophetics can frustrate the orderly or systematic person. Although their intuitive insights usually occur well in advance of actual events, Prophetics often get last-minute insights or suggestions that can change your whole plan. You may find yourself thinking or saying, "Why didn't you tell me this sooner?" Try not to overreact: Prophetics can't, because they seldom rigidly plan ahead. They know ideas will come to them when they need them.

By the same token, Prophetics often will interrupt you halfway through a statement and say, "I know . . ." They aren't being rude or presumptuous. They really *do* know what you are about to say, or what you mean, before you finish saying it, thanks to their combined intuition and quick-mindedness. Instead of taking offense, try to enjoy this time-saving feature. If you try to slow down a Prophetic, he or she is likely to tune you out mentally.

When I watch auras I can always spot a Prophetic who is bored by a plodding conversational partner. The Prophetic's attention will be focused on the speaker for a moment. Then a purple flash will streak out from the Prophetic's aura—indicating that he or she has leaped to some other interesting thought until the partner has reached a new conversational point. The moral: When talking to a Prophetic, keep it short and quick if you want to hold their attention. On a humorous note, nothing is more fascinating than listening to two Prophetics talking to each other. You will notice that they never finish their sentences. The entire conversation is conducted in a sort of psychic shorthand as they "uh-huh" and "I know" back and forth.

Prophetics are creatures of two extremes. As we have seen, their intuitive ideas may occur well in advance of events. Yet they also have many last-minute insights and suggestions. What is missing is the work in the middle. To Prophetics, that "middle" part—getting from insight to action—is boring. If you are a highly organized person and do things step by step, you may find you are doing that part of the work by yourself. The moral: Never delegate detail work to a Prophetic—it simply won't get done. Don't try to force them to do it with you, either, for their playfulness will distract you. Whether it's thinking about the future or what to do at the moment, spontaneity is the key word for Prophetics. Don't try to force them to make or hold to a rigid plan. Allow them the freedom to think of creative ideas for a current project one minute and muse about many possible futures the next. They handle this rapid shifting of gears with no difficulty. Prophetics are usually reading several books at a time and always have as many irons in the fire as possible.

Prophetics are the spice of life. Prophetics always know "what's happening"—where the latest lecture, recital, seminar, or party is taking place. They constantly seek out new diversions. Being with them, even for a short while, can broaden your horizons and enrich your life. Because they want to know everything . . . because they constantly seek new ideas and information . . . they make the life of those around them lively and interesting. If you have Prophetic friends, your life will be hectic but seldom dull. If you stop to think about it you will realize that the person who first interested you in psychic phenomena, or who first told you about this book, is probably a Prophetic. Return the favor by developing your own Psychic Intuition and sharing what you have learned with others.

As you have learned, Psychic Intuition is the most unlimited of the four psychic senses. That means that the more you practice using it, the more whole dimensions of psychic skills and practical lifestyle advantages will open to you. As we have also seen, however, intuition is spontaneous and may not give us the full perspective so necessary for mature judgment.

That perspective is often provided by the next of the psychic senses we will explore, Psychic Hearing. There is a logical progression from knowing to hearing. People tend to confuse the two at times because both have an inner mental quality. But Psychic Hearing can serve as a sort of inner computer, a way to analyze the insights of Psychic Intuition. In the next chapter you will learn how to tap the secrets of that analyzing computer.

(The answers to Self-Test 3 are, in order, A, C, B, and D.)

The Gift of Prophecy—Psychic Intuition

ADVANTAGES

Quickest of the psychic senses (just "knowing" intuitively)
Best psychic sense for early warning
Best for psychically sensing the future
Best psychic sense for remote scanning
Most unlimited of the psychic senses

DISADVANTAGES

Impressions are fleeting and sometimes hard to capture
Impressions frequently come with no other supporting information
Hardest psychic sense to trust initially

People High in Psychic Intuition

STRENGTHS

Excellent anticipators of problems or difficulties
Quick-minded and can adjust rapidly to changing circumstances
Naturally sense how to be at the right place at the right time
Do not waste time worrying needlessly
Are innovators with limitless creativity and are seldom restricted by convention
Instinctively know the needs of family members and loved ones
Hate to miss anything and love a good party

WEAKNESSES

Can be scattered by the volume of thoughts and ideas they receive
Pick up information far in advance and sometimes too soon
Are easily bored and frequently don't complete a project
Are often ahead of other people's timing and are resented for it
Can speak too quickly, blurting out what comes to mind without thinking it over first

• 4 •

Psychic Hearing—The Voice That Speaks Within

FOR MOST PEOPLE a fever that climbs above 99 degrees is usually no more than an early warning signal of incipient illness. For Richard, such a temperature can be an immediate threat to his life. After doctors removed Richard's diseased pituitary gland, they explained to his wife that he would no longer be able to adjust to even the slightest touch of fever, since the pituitary controls the internal thermostat that regulates body temperature.

Marsha was just glad that the surgery went well and that her husband was home from the hospital. But one morning when Richard awoke he told his wife he felt as if he were "coming down with something." When Marsha took his temperature it registered 98.7 degrees—a mere one-tenth of a degree above normal. She fussed a bit trying to make Richard more comfortable but her attentions seemed to irritate him. Never a cooperative convalescent, he wanted to be left alone.

Reluctantly, Marsha went about her morning's routine, trying not to worry about her husband. Suddenly a voice in her mind exploded: *"Check Richard now!"* she heard it shout. She rushed into the bedroom to find her husband burning with fever, eyes unfocused, semiconscious. Over his mumbled protests Marsha half dragged, half carried Richard to the car and drove to the hospital's emergency room. By the time they got there Richard's temperature was 103 degrees and rising. Later, when his condition was under control, the doctors told Marsha that had she delayed even fifteen minutes, her husband would have died.

Marsha's Psychic Hearing—her inner voice—had saved Richard's life.

All the psychic senses can alert you to danger. Psychic Feeling functions as a sort of "body radar." With Psychic Intuition you "know" that trouble lies ahead. Psychic Vision, as we shall discover, helps you to see and thus avoid potential problems. But a warning via Psychic Hearing really grabs your attention in a way none of the others can. You may pass off a feeling as nervousness; an intuition as anxiety or worry; a vision as just your imagination. But Psychic Hearing— especially at full volume, the way Marsha experienced it—is an extrasensory experience impossible to ignore. Could you ignore someone talking or shouting inside your head?

An experience like Marsha's is a bit unusual; it occurs only when a situation is dangerous in the extreme, or when a loved one is involved. Most of the time, however, Psychic Hearing impressions (sometimes also called clairaudience) are gentle and subtle, like hearing quiet music or a muted voice that speaks to you through stereo headphones.

That inside-the-head sensation is what makes Psychic Hearing so much like talking to yourself. Unfortunately, it also creates what we might call a "credibility gap" for people who are high in this psychic sense. They don't think of themselves as having ESP and tend to ask:

- Does psychic perception really exist?

• Why haven't I had the same kind and number of ESP experiences as other people?

• Others have strong feelings, experience intuitive premonitions, see visions. Why doesn't that happen to me?

Are these the kind of questions you have asked yourself? Perhaps you have had an inner dialogue along the lines of *"Maybe I'm not psychic"* . . . *"Maybe I'm not doing something right—all I experience is hearing myself think"* . . . *"My premonitions are just mental judgments based on what I already understand."*

If you have asked yourself those questions and come to those conclusions, it's highly likely that you are high in Psychic Hearing but do not recognize or understand how to utilize your psychic strengths. You do not realize you have been and are having valid psychic experiences.

Take heart. You can learn to develop your particular form of ESP. In this chapter you will learn about the still, small voice that speaks within you. You will learn how it works for you all the time. You will learn how that voice can give you good advice, help you to analyze yourself creatively, and guide you to success in life. Most important, you will learn why being analytical is natural for you.

Does the mental dialogue outlined above sound like something someone you live with might say? No doubt you've had a hard time convincing that person that ESP does exist. You've probably found him or her highly skeptical. Be patient; that behavior is typical of people high in Psychic Hearing.

Clairaudient People Need to Understand

Psychic Hearing involves the reception of extrasensory signals as a word, a sound, or some form of language. A clairaudient impression is an inner hearing, often quite similar to what you hear in your mind when you talk to yourself.

In its gentler forms clairaudience can be as subtle as a mental understanding that comes in language form.

Because Psychic Hearing manifests itself as inner mental dialogue, people high in this form of ESP do not feel satisfied until they completely understand. That is what makes them so analytical. They want to hear and understand to be *sure.* This gives them the sense of clarity and precision they require, just as the Feeler needs to feel comfortable and the Visionary needs to see. With that analytical nature, however, they can easily talk themselves out of their ESP.

A Scientist Proves It to Himself

Because Psychic Hearing is so close to thinking to yourself, many Audients do not realize when they are hearing psychically. They assume they are merely thinking out loud. Actually, their mind has bounced a thought off the universe and they are receiving an "echo"—a psychic response—via clairaudience. Those who are strong in Psychic Hearing become so used to this psychic echo that it becomes second nature to them; they do not think of it as ESP, nor regard themselves as psychic, even when the truth stares them in the face. Consider the story of a Free Soul student of mine which illustrates how clairaudient individuals can receive psychic impressions without realizing what they are doing.

Clifford, a research biologist and oceanographer, came to investigate ESP after his wife was killed in an accident. Her sudden passing meant he had not been able to say a final goodbye to her. Twice while his wife lay in a coma he mentally heard her silently call his name and speak to him. Clifford desperately wanted to believe the communication was real, and grief finally overcame his scientific skepticism. Even though he could recall having no other examples of psychic perception, from his description of the incident it was apparent that Psychic Hearing was one of Clifford's strengths. Yet each time he had some success with psychic techniques Clifford would doubt himself, or claim it was "just coincidence."

Finally, in a class on Psychic Hearing, students were asked to get clairaudient impressions of their classmates, to stand in front of each one and see what word, inner phrase, or sentence came to them that would identify something about the individual they faced. Clifford resisted any suggestion that he'd had a valid psychic experience. He did admit receiving impressions during the experiment, but felt that since he knew the people he was working with, his impressions were simply those of his logical mind reasoning out words and phrases that described what he already thought about them. "In fact," Clifford said, "it seems pointless to continue since I know everyone in the group—except that lady over there."

That lady—Joanne—proved to be the perfect person to help Clifford prove to himself that he was in fact psychic, thanks to the mix of roles she filled in her life. Joanne had recently had her first child, a daughter, and was glowing with the joy of motherhood. Professionally, she was a lawyer. On top of all this she had recently managed her husband's successful campaign for public office.

I devised a test to convince Clifford. Taking Joanne aside, I told her to send three different messages to him. First, she was to radiate the warmth and love she felt when she was mothering her daughter. Next, she was to assume her lawyer role and think of the type of activities her work involved. Third, she was to think about her part in the political campaign.

All Clifford knew was that he was supposed to try sensing Joanne three separate times. When the test was over Clifford said skeptically, "Now I know I'm not psychic because I got three totally different impressions. First I heard a lullaby in my mind and a soothing voice talking, like to a baby. Next I had the sense that my mind was working in legalistic terms. Finally I heard the phrase, *'Her husband better know who's the boss!'*"

When I explained to Clifford the test I had set up his mouth dropped open. I said, "See, you *are* psychic. Now stop trying to talk yourself out of it and start learning to develop your natural Psychic Hearing."

Clifford's skepticism is common to many people high in Psychic Hearing. Because the impressions they receive are so close to their own thoughts, they do not separate the two. They have been using that inner psychic echo for so long, and it is so interwoven with their own thinking process, that they take it for granted, not realizing that it can be a major source of psychic information.

The Hearing Psychic Reception Area

Both Psychic Hearing and that inner dialogue use the same wiring and internal sound system. The speaker is the Psychic Reception Area for clairaudience. It is located on either side of the head above ear level. This section of the skull lies over that part of the brain called the temporal lobes. It is an area of the cerebrum that processes auditory information. Here nerve signals from the inner ear are gathered, sorted, and integrated so that sound waves striking the ear drum can be perceived as words or language.

The pioneer American brain surgeon, the late Dr. Wilder Penfield, found in the 1950s that electrically stimulating portions of the temporal lobes during surgery caused his patients to hear music or remember bits of conversation. Focusing your attention directly in this temporal-lobe area above the level of the ears seems to bypass the need to receive hearing information as sound waves. Words and language are simply mentally understood. In contrast, focusing

Figure #3   The Hearing Psychic Reception Area

at ear level is what you do naturally when you want to use your physical hearing more acutely (as at that cocktail party I described in Chapter 1) if you want to hear that across-the-room conversation more clearly.

Focusing *at* ear level seems to inhibit Psychic Hearing. The key to tapping Psychic Hearing is to direct your attention above the ears. Which side you focus on does not matter. In fact, if you put your listening attention inside your head rather than toward a specific side, you are more likely to have clairaudient success. Let's practice tapping the Hearing Psychic Reception Area with a warm-up exercise:

1. Sit comfortably; relax.
2. Take a deep breath and exhale gently.

3. Practice sensing the different parts of your head area. Without touching them, be aware of your ears and the level of your ears.

4. Now shift your focus upward and sense the area above your ears. Be aware of the sides of your head one or two inches above ear level.

5. Note how this area has a heightened sensitivity, like a microphone ready to amplify any sound or signal. Picture huge megaphones channeling psychic vibration directly to the temporal lobes.

6. Alternate the levels of focus several times, first aiming your awareness at ear level, then letting it slide up to the temporal-lobe area above the ears.

Now let's practice noticing the difference between outer and inner listening that I described earlier. Move to a location where you can hear people talking around you; sit down and relax.

• Listen to some background conversation. Notice how your attention is not only at ear level, but how your sense of the sound is outside of you, distant.

• Shift your focus now to the temporal-lobe area and talk to yourself, think to yourself. Notice how your attention is not only above ear level, but how your focus is inward rather than outward.

These two processes are the keys to being able to tap Psychic Hearing at will. Knowing how to shift your attention above ear level and how to focus your awareness inward are the skills that make clairaudience accessible on command. Practicing this inner form of listening also helps turn up the volume on your Psychic Hearing. This gives you the added benefit of opening a new source of psychic feedback when you talk to yourself, since you can use your clairaudience to receive psychic echoes from the universe when you mentally pose a question or need to solve a problem. Here is an example.

Good Advice from the Voice Within

Like many modern women, Marybeth Spain, a Free Soul instructor in Vienna, Virginia, faces the daily challenges of balancing a career and motherhood. A faculty member at George Mason University with a Ph.D. in Russian literature, Marybeth juggles the pressures of college teaching and the stresses of coping with her rambunctious sons, ages eight and four. Complicating Marybeth's situation even further is the fact that her husband travels out of the country for weeks at a time for his work as a health educator in Third World countries. "When he is away, the added pressure can trigger one tension headache after another," Marybeth told me.

One day several years ago the pressures of Marybeth's dual role seemed about to break her. Her husband had been in Pakistan for two weeks; she had a mountain of exam papers to correct; and, because it was raining, her two boys were constantly underfoot demanding her attention. She could feel a tension headache starting to build. Since Marybeth had recently completed Free Soul training, she decided to try to relax through the meditation techniques she had learned. She closed her eyes and thought, "What can I do to make today bearable? How can I be there for my children and still get my work done?"

Marybeth is naturally strong in Psychic Hearing. As soon as she silently voiced her thoughts she heard the clairaudient echo response: *"Relax . . . make a game of the day. . . . Take the papers to the enclosed porch and let the boys play near you while you work."* Marybeth felt that a tremendous weight had been lifted from her shoulders. Though it took her nearly all day to finish marking her students' papers, her headache disappeared and she actually enjoyed the time. The peace of mind she got from watching the rain through the porch windows refreshed her spirit. "How different it was from my usual pattern," she said. Clearly, consulting her psychic inner voice improved the quality of Marybeth's life. She now uses the process regularly to find creative solutions to other problems that stem from the conflict of motherhood and career.

Tapping Your Creative Analysis Abilities

Just as Marybeth used clairaudience to find an answer to her question, so you can develop your Psychic Hearing channel for controlled meditation. Take a moment and practice this form of psychic echoing; see how you can best use it to find answers to questions that may trouble you. Start with something simple. Shift your focus to the temporal-lobe area and mentally ask yourself the following questions. Note any response you hear, or any words or phrases that come to your mind. Jot them down. Remember to write down your first impression. Don't analyze it yet; just record it.

- What are my good points?
- What are my weaknesses?
- In what ways am I learning to deal with my weaknesses?
- How can I use my good points and strengths to make further progress?

How did you do? Did you notice how quick and easy it was to get responses? Review what you wrote. Observe how valid and constructive your impressions were. Learning to tap the Hearing Psychic Reception Area can be tremendously helpful in any form of meditation or creative thinking. Most people have difficulty with problem-solving meditation; they know how to ask the questions, but they don't know where to listen for the answers. When you learn to tap Psychic Hearing on command, you are able to tune in to psychic echoes as they return to you from the universe. You can, in effect, learn to become your own counselor by using this form of ESP.

Psychic Guidewords: Psychic Hearing Keys for Success

The value of Psychic Hearing doesn't stop with the benefits of self-counseling and self-teaching. When you learn to bounce that psychic echo off the people and events around you, you can put Psychic Hearing to even greater usefulness.

For instance, one of the most practical uses of ESP in daily life is getting key guidewords through Psychic Hearing. In the same way that you asked questions about yourself and received a psychic echo response, you can ask questions about people and situations in your life and receive in return psychic guidewords that offer key insights for communicating and acting most effectively. I use this technique in almost everything I do, and the guidewords help me determine how best to approach any situation. It is particularly effective when I use it before giving a radio, television, or newspaper interview. It helps me tune in to the interviewers.

Once, while preparing for a newspaper interview in Denver, I mentally asked myself how best to approach the reporter. I clearly heard the reply in my mind: *"Answer any questions she asks."* When I tried to pick up other keywords, phrases, or insights, I got nothing. That one phrase echoed again and again.

My interviewer was a charming young woman. She seemed friendly and totally captivated by the exploration of psychic phenomena from a scientific point of view. When we started, however, she proceeded to ask me question after question about my childhood and early upbringing. For more than half an hour she continued to probe areas that seemed to me to have little or nothing to do with the substance of our interview.

I grew increasingly anxious as I watched our time tick away with nothing that I felt was of real importance being covered. Yet all I could do was trust the Psychic Hearing I

had received: *"Answer any questions she asks."* So I continued to be honest and forthright, responding to what seemed
to me to be a line of inquiry completely off the track. Finally,
after more than forty minutes, the reporter took her pad and
ripped out the pages of notes she had taken. To my horror,
she threw them into the wastebasket. Then she said, "Now I
feel I know you, and from your answers I feel I can trust you.
Let's begin the real interview." That interview is one of the
best I've had appear in print.

Even more striking is a meeting I had with a well-known
and controversial talk-radio host in New York City. Tuning in
to my Psychic Hearing before we met, I mentally asked: "How
should I behave? What can I expect? How can I best reach
this man?" Shifting up to the Hearing Psychic Reception Area
after each question, I heard the answers: *"Don't be intimi-
dated. Don't let anything surprise you or throw you off-
guard."* And finally, *"Interrupt him. Cut him off if he makes
even one inaccurate statement."*

The first two impressions made sense, because I knew
about the host's penchant for attacking his guests. The third
really seemed a formula for disaster, especially in light of
how the interview began. To intimidate a guest, the host
refused to meet you until just moments before air time.
Guests were kept waiting without even the briefest of greet-
ings from any member of the production staff. Worse yet, as
I walked into the studio set seconds before the interview
was to begin, the host threw my assistant out. He scowled at
me, implying that I had violated his territory by even thinking
about bringing another person into the studio. In seeming
punishment, the host ignored me for the next ten minutes
while he told his listeners, "I think I'll answer some more
calls before we get to our next guest."

When the interview finally got under way I was assaulted
with one of the most negative tirades I've ever experienced
on radio. "You don't look like a kook," my talk-radio host
said. "Your background doesn't seem like one a weirdo would

have. So how did you get involved in this way-out, shady field?" From the way I'd been treated so far, my interviewer didn't seem like a man it would be wise to interrupt and further irritate. But I recalled the last Psychic Hearing impression I had received: *"Interrupt him. Don't let him get away with the smallest misrepresentation."*

In the first five minutes of our session I cut off the host more times than in all my previous media appearances combined. At every turn, before he could build up a head of negative remarks, I interrupted and forced him to confront the facts. I presented the latest scientific studies and discussed practical approaches to ESP with an overassertiveness that had me virtually taking charge of the program. I couldn't believe what I was doing. At the time I thought, "Well, this is really trusting your psychic impressions and practicing what you preach!" The result? The bombast stopped, the tirades slowed down. The negative skepticism turned from mindless attack to "I don't know what to make of you. What you're saying seems to make sense." At the end of the interview the host told our listeners, "Folks, I think I'm going to attend this man's lecture after all." Incidentally, the success of these two interviews led to lecture appearances that attracted more than twice the usual audience.

You, too, can use psychic keywords to guide you successfully in daily life. All it takes is the discipline to tune in ahead of time. Here are specifics to remember when getting these psychic keywords:

• Ten to fifteen minutes before meeting someone is usually the best time to tune in.

• Hold the person and circumstance in mind by picturing, feeling, or thinking about them, whichever is more natural for you.

• Mentally ask questions like: How can I best approach this person or situation? What are my keys to success? What should I be wary of? What should I avoid?

In each case note the thought, word, or phrase that comes to you after you silently ask the question.

• *Don't try. Don't force.* Think the question, focus on that Hearing Psychic Reception Area, and note what words or phrases come to mind.

• Be sure to write down the answers, or make a mental note of them and review them just before your meeting.

Receiving Your Own Mantra

Getting a daily mantra is another way you can use Psychic Hearing for greater success in life. *Mantra* is a Sanskrit term for a word or phrase to be chanted or intoned as a prayer or guiding vibration. Being in tune with your mantra is supposed to bring your life into harmony with your spiritual aspect and thus make you happier and more successful. Westerners have been exposed to the concept of a mantra through various Eastern religions and organizations that recommend chanting a mantra as part of meditation.

Actually, a mantra is nothing more than a Psychic Hearing keyword for yourself. You can receive a different and specific mantra every day once you know how to tap the Hearing Psychic Reception Area. Why pay someone to give you your mantra when you can get it yourself for any day, week, month, or even for a single specific event? Using that Psychic Hearing echo to receive your mantra guideword is an extrasensory way to determine what frame of mind, or vibration, is best for you that day. Remember, a mantra does not always have to be deeply spiritual or esoteric. Daily mantras are often down to earth and practical. Consider this example:

Robert, a self-employed businessman in Washington, D.C., meditates each morning to receive his keyword mantra for the day. He told me not long ago how one mantra in particular saved him money. On the day in question he clearly heard, *"Don't wait!"* as he tapped the Hearing Psychic Reception Area for his keyword. Next, he thought of the friends he was to meet later to finish planning their joint skiing vacation. He heard, *"Don't listen to them."*

Robert and his wife had planned on flying with the other couple and their children to the New Hampshire cabin they were going to share. The four had been making their plans for weeks. Usually when Robert meditated or got a mantra for the day, he received phrases such as *"Be patient"* or *"Stay flexible."* For that reason the mantra he heard this time stood out. He carefully wrote it down. Later that day Robert heard a radio commercial for a special airline fare. As it grabbed his attention his keyword—*"Don't wait!"*—flashed to mind. Without hesitation the usually unspontaneous Robert picked up the phone and made reservations for the reduced-fare tickets for himself, his wife, and his son. Robert encouraged his friends to act quickly and do the same, but they said they would wait a day until they could check out the deal with their travel agent. Robert, remembering the *"Don't listen to them"* part of his mantra, decided to buy his tickets right away.

The next day Washington was paralyzed by a foot and a half of snow. Roads were impassable. Offices were closed. Businesses didn't open. Robert's friends had to wait three days before a snowplow could make it down their residential side street. By the time they finally could contact their travel agent all the airlines had discontinued special fares. By following his mantra that day Robert saved more than $300.

The Practical Five-Minute Morning Meditation

Most of us don't have the luxury of a half-hour or an hour for a complicated morning meditation. Here is a simple step-by-step process you can use to enhance the success of your day with guidewords and mantras. All it takes is a few minutes before you start your day's activities. Let's try it now and also practice getting your own mantra.

1. Sit quietly and relax.
2. As you breathe comfortably and easily, turn your thoughts inward and focus on yourself and your day.
3. Project the mental question and at the same time let it echo in your mind, "What approach or vibration is best for me today?" (If it is late in the day, ask about tomorrow.)
4. Grasp and note the word, phrase, or understanding that comes to your mind.
5. Continue the process by reviewing the people and events of your upcoming day and getting psychic guidewords for dealing with them.

One way to prove your Psychic Hearing skills, and to realize the value of getting guidewords and mantras, is to write them down daily and see how they have helped you.

Signals from the Psychic Hearing Orchestra

Now that you've been introduced to the uses of Psychic Hearing and the techniques for tapping it on command, let's explore other extrasensory experiences that serve as an indicator of Psychic Hearing sensitivity. You may be more clairaudient than you know.

- Hearing your name called without its actually being spoken
- Hearing "between the lines"—something that radiates psychically though no one actually says it
- Hearing a song in your mind that provides insights or information

- Talking to yourself and getting useful "echo" answers
- Projecting thoughts other people can psychically hear

Each of these examples also offers insights into some of the characteristics of the Audient psychic personality.

Hearing your name called without its actually being spoken:

Psychic Hearing is the extrasensory channel most people identify with mental telepathy—with reading another person's mind or hearing another's thoughts. Actually, any of the four psychic senses can be used to get an impression of what someone is thinking, but hearing those thoughts is what most people regard as true telepathy. Hearing your name called is a common example of a striking though minor experience with this type of thought transference.

Each of us is uniquely tuned to our own name. In a room where a dozen conversations may be going on simultaneously, we naturally perk up our ears and turn in the direction of someone who mentions our name. The brain seems to have a special sensitivity to sound waves that form the pattern of our name. Whenever that particular pattern reaches our eardrums, our attention is automatically drawn to it. That response holds true for psychic frequencies as well. Of all the thoughts that people radiate, those involving our name are likely to catch our psychic attention. Paying attention to that psychic name-calling can often be useful.

While on Navy service in the Mediterranean, my ship was in port at Cannes during that city's annual film festival. I was standing on deck enjoying the view of the many luxurious yachts anchored nearby when I heard the captain call my name. I could not see him anywhere. Thinking the call might be a psychic page rather than a vocal one, I went to the captain's cabin, where I found him talking with George Peppard, the actor, who had asked if he could tour our ship. The captain was looking for someone to show the actor around. When I spoke with the captain later, he said my showing up at his cabin at that moment was certainly a coincidence, because he had been thinking of summoning me. But he was going to use the first junior officer he could find to be the actor's guide.

That psychic page gave me a thoroughly rewarding experience—a chance to meet an actor whose work I enjoyed (not to mention complimentary tickets to one of the film festival's screenings).

This story illustrates two key characteristics of people strong in Psychic Hearing. First, they tend to be mentally alert and quick to react. Second, their initiative usually leads to new opportunities. Audients don't wait for things to happen; they make them happen. They are the go-getters and early birds who frequently get the worm (or, in this case, the tickets).

Hearing "between the lines"—something that radiates psychically though no one actually says it:
Because Psychic Hearing is the form of ESP most closely interwoven with physical hearing, the two are likely to occur simultaneously. A person high in Psychic Hearing often picks up mental impressions as he or she listens to someone speak. Their psychic attention is attracted not so much by what is said, as by something beyond the sounds and words. It is, in effect, a sort of second dialogue that takes place between the lines of the spoken conversation. In one instance, at least, the strength of these psychic signals saved a life.

Rebecca, a Chicago social worker, frequently uses Psychic Hearing to listen to the inner turmoil that the adolescents she works with are often unable to express. Recently her Psychic Hearing—her ability to listen between the lines— saved a young girl from taking her own life. The incident had its beginnings when Rebecca read an article in a high school newspaper. Amy, a sixteen-year-old who had recently attempted suicide, wrote bitterly about how little help she had gotten from a crisis hotline. Amy felt trapped at home and desperately wanted to get away, she wrote, but the hotline counselors couldn't aid her because, as a minor, she needed the permission of her father (her only living parent). Amy's sense of helplessness resulted in a depression that led to her ineffective suicide attempt. Amy ended her article by saying she was now fully recovered, back in school, adjusted to waiting out the two years that remained before she would graduate and be independent.

The words in the article said everything was fine. But the voice Rebecca heard behind those words signaled just the opposite. It was as if Amy were speaking to her directly, and the tones and inflections were all wrong. What Rebecca heard in that inner mental voice was not a recovered and adjusted young woman but a bitter, despondent, and still deeply disturbed girl in trouble. Rebecca was so sure of her psychic sensing that she went to Amy's school and asked to speak with the girl. Amy insisted everything was all right, but Rebecca wouldn't give up. Finally her persistence paid off: Amy gradually revealed a story of years of mental and physical abuse by her father.

Amy had told the hotline counselors only that she was unhappy at home. She didn't tell them that her father belt-whipped her weekly, and often made her kneel on the floor on hard grains of rice for hours at a time. Armed with this information, Rebecca was able to get in touch with protective services. Eventually a court sent Amy to a safe shelter. Amy feels Rebecca's intervention saved her from a second (and possibly successful) suicide attempt by hearing her psychic cry for help.

Like many people high in Psychic Hearing, Rebecca is persistent and pursues what she wants to fully understand. The things Amy said in the article just didn't match what Rebecca heard and understood in her mind. Like a dog with a bone, Rebecca kept chewing on the problem until she broke through to the core of the issue.

Hearing a song in your mind that provides insights or information:

Gloria's story (in Chapter 1) is an example of this variation of clairaudience. In that instance, Gloria heard the song immediately after she had mentally asked a question, so its meaning was quite clear to her. But in some cases the song is meant to be a more general message and at other times it is not so much the lyrics as it is the melody and emotional associations one has with the song that provide psychic insight.

For Tom, a Free Soul student, the key was the emotional response triggered by Olivia Newton-John's song, "Got to Believe We Are Magic." Tom had moved to the West Coast from Nebraska hoping to write television and film scripts. Like many who seek success in Hollywood, he set out full of dreams and confidence, but they faded soon after he arrived in California. There was the cultural shock of moving from a rural farming community to the complex Los Angeles sprawl. The inaccessibility of writers, directors, and producers added to Tom's frustration and growing self-doubt. When in one week three agents refused to take him as a client, his self-esteem hit rock bottom.

Tom was ready to give up and head home when he heard that a television sitcom producer was looking for a writer with a country background. He thought about trying to get the job, but was too despondent to do anything about it. At that point Tom couldn't take another rejection. Suddenly he seemed to hear *"Got to Believe We Are Magic"* running through his mind. It wouldn't stop. As the words *"nothing can stand in our way"* echoed inside his mind, Tom felt as if a guardian-angel muse was telling him to believe in himself.

From that moment, Tom's attitude started to change. His self-doubt began to fade, his self-confidence was renewed. He no longer thought of the sitcom job-opening as a source of rejection; he now viewed it as a challenge he could make into an adventure. Totally caught up in the spirit of believing in his own magic, Tom drove to the producer's office and told the secretary to announce him as "the literary giant from Fremont, Nebraska." The producer was so amused by Tom's approach that he saw him without an appointment and eventually offered Tom the job. This story, aside from showing how a psychically heard tune can turn a life around, also illustrates another characteristic of Audient people: They are outstanding at bouncing back quickly. In addition to the perseverance that both Tom and Rebecca displayed, Audients tend not to stay depressed for long. Sometimes just a single word or thought is enough to give them new hope and initiative. Psychic Hearing provides the perfect channel.

Talking to yourself and getting useful "echo" answers:

People high in Psychic Hearing experience a constant inner dialogue. Because they tend to think in words, they solve problems by asking questions and hearing answers rather than by seeing a picture, getting a feeling, or having an intuitive knowing. The desire to hear an answer is what leads Audients to ask themselves so many internal questions, and to trust the voice within, the psychic responses they hear. So far we've seen Psychic Hearing at work in dramatic ways—saving a child's life, renewing a man's career. But it can be useful, too, in more humble ways—such as locating a set of misplaced car keys.

Maureen and her husband, Don, live in an outer suburb of Denver. One morning Don couldn't find his car keys. Because Maureen had used his car the day before, Don was sure she had misplaced them. Since he had to get to work, Don took his wife's car, leaving her stranded at home. Maureen clearly recalled putting the keys on the dining room table; she was sure Don had picked them up. Who was at fault was a moot point, however. Maureen had to find the keys if she wanted to be able to get to work herself.

Calmly, Maureen closed her eyes and mentally asked,

"How can I find the keys?" In her Hearing Psychic Reception Area she heard *"Take the dog and go to the park."* Since Smokey needed to be walked anyway, and a search of the house had turned up nothing, she decided she might as well go to the park. On the way she wondered why she had received that strange answer. Once again her psychic inner voice responded: *"Because the keys are there."*

Once in the park Smokey followed his normal sniffing trail that led to the playground. As they neared the swings Maureen spotted the keys beside one of the poles. She realized they must have fallen out of Don's jacket pocket when he walked Smokey the night before.

Maureen is typical of Audients. They don't get rattled or overemotional when faced with a problem, but tackle it step by step. Whether you call it logic or psychic perception, the voice within helps them to handle crises, either large or small.

Projecting thoughts other people can psychically hear:

Strongly Audient men and women not only receive clairaudient impressions, they also project them. Their logical minds and emphasis on language make it easier for them to transmit thoughts that others can psychically hear. This is called *thought projection,* another example of mental telepathy that involves Psychic Hearing. If an Audient's thoughts are strong enough, the receiver can hear them as words or phrases, as a subliminal psychic message.

Ralph is particularly gifted in Psychic Hearing. A middle-aged professional, he is powerfully built and has an intense personality to match. Mentally and physically, he radiates energy. When Ralph and his wife, Doris, were looking for a home in a scenic location near a national forest, they knew their choices were limited. One house, in a particularly beautiful canyon, seemed ideal. But optimism turned to disappointment when they found that the inside of the house didn't offer the floor plan or views they wanted. As the couple were leaving, the owner pointed out his own home nearby. Something about it grabbed Ralph instantly. He thought, *"Let us know if you ever decide to sell it,"* but that seemed so presumptuous an idea that Ralph said nothing out loud.

Two months later Ralph was away on a business trip when he got a call from Doris. The owner had suddenly decided to sell his home, and had phoned before putting it on the market. Why? Because, the owner said, "I remember hearing you ask to have the first option on buying it!" Ralph's thoughts had been so strong that the owner had picked them up.

Such experiences are not uncommon. Audient people tend to radiate an intense amount of mental energy. When those thought patterns are amplified by emotions or strong desire, the signals are doubly strong. If those around Audients are psychically receptive, they will hear or understand the thoughts. People high in Psychic Intuition seem to be the most receptive. Many people, particularly those who are very psychically sensitive often experience an Audient's mental bombardment as pressure, or as an energy field that makes them want to back away. This is why Psychic Feelers and Prophetics sometimes find the company of people high in Psychic Hearing unpleasant, and may feel Audients themselves to be pushy and overaggressive.

Understanding the Strength of the Audient Personality

If you have friends or colleagues who are high in Psychic Hearing, expect them to come on strong in their interaction with you. Don't be offended, and don't take it personally. Powerful mental energy is natural for Audients; moreover, they are less sensitive in Psychic Feeling and do not realize how overwhelming their energy can be. And since Audients prefer clear mental hearing rather than the subtleties of inner feelings or intuitions, they have their volume set on high most of the time. Strong mental projection helps them get the strong feedback they need in order to be sure of the response.

Whether it is a psychic echo or your physical response to them, Audients want to know exactly what the message is. They want things direct, clear, understandable. In much the same way a tourist abroad thinks that by speaking loudly to a taxi driver the driver will understand English better, so Audient people turn up their personality volume when they want to be understood. If you are high in Psychic Hearing and reflect the Audient's mental assertiveness, be more aware of your effect on others. Watch to see if they back away from you. Notice if friends frequently complain that you have hurt their feelings. If you find that people shy away when you speak with them, try directing your energy and words off to the side rather than straight at them. However, don't feel guilty or try to change yourself. Just realize that what to you is normal assertiveness may be too much for other people. Do not expect them to value the same thinking processes or direct approaches you do.

Listening for the Audient People Around You

"What's your reasoning?" "I just don't understand!" "Why can't you explain it to me?" "Don't talk to me about feelings; let's discuss this logically!" "Prove it to me; where are the facts?" "I don't care how you feel, just get it done!" These are some of the calling cards of the Audient personality. Locating the Audients around you is as easy as hearing a tank approach in the woods. Little about them is subtle. Physically and psychically, Audient people give a new meaning to the word *assertive.* Once they have reasoned out their opinion or idea, they are never bashful in presenting it. Audients apply the full strength of their will to any project. To them, tact and diplomacy only tend to confuse clear communication and understanding.

When Audients have not made up their minds on an issue, they will ask countless questions until they fully understand your point of view—or until they drive you crazy, whichever comes first. They want to hear all the pertinent data. Choose your responses carefully, however. Keyed to language and hearing, Audients take your words literally, and hold you to them. If you say you will meet them at noon, arriving at 12:05 P.M. will be seen as not keeping your word. Telling an Audient "I'll handle it" means "It will get done no matter what," not "I'll try my best." After all, that is the way Audients approach life.

Keys to Success with Audient People and Psychic Hearing

Understanding the way Audients think is imperative in order to avoid overreacting to them. How can you better understand and get along with Audients? Listen to them. Listen to the questions they ask and you will hear what their logical minds are seeking to understand. Listen to them as they make statements and you will hear what they expect of you. Listen psychically, and you will hear the Audients' inner plea: "Understand and accept me as I am!"

Practice clairaudience in order to get the keywords that will help you deal with Audients. Practice is also the best way to develop your own Psychic Hearing and mind-reading ability. Since Psychic Hearing is frequently our least-developed ESP channel, it makes sense to tune in to those who are its most forceful transmitters. The more you practice, the more adept you will become. Soon, getting keywords and mental insights for the people you deal with will become second nature. Tapping Psychic Hearing to get a daily mantra will come easily. And best of all, you will develop an inner computer that can tap the psychic echoes of the universe for information and understanding.

The Gift of Psychic Hearing

ADVANTAGES

At full volume, the best for grabbing your attention
Best for getting key guidewords and initial direction
Best for understanding and analyzing a problem or situation
Best psychic sense for thought projection
Best for getting specific answers to questions

DISADVANTAGES

At low volume, can be confused with your own thoughts
One of the slower psychic senses
One of the hardest psychic senses to develop

People High in Psychic Hearing

STRENGTHS

Can hear when someone is lying to them
Are the best at getting keyword mantras
Are the best transmitters of psychic thoughts
Are least likely to experience psychic overload
Are direct, uncomplicated initiators

Are excellent organizers of details
Are the best at receiving and understanding specific psychic
  information

WEAKNESSES/THINGS TO BE AWARE OF

Can doubt their psychic potential and talk themselves out of
  ESP
Can be overanalytical and ask too many questions
Can come on too strong and radiate too much mental energy
Can have trouble trusting feelings and intuition
Can be least sensitive to psychic subtleties

· 5 ·

Psychic Vision— The World of Clairvoyance

THE DAY was clear and cold, but Sheila and her two young sons, warm inside the family car, sang to the car radio's music as she drove north on the New England Thruway. Traffic was sparse, the roadway was dry—but suddenly a vision appeared to Sheila. In her mind's eye she saw an accident, and saw herself veering sharply right to avoid the car that seemed to loom in front of her. Sheila was jolted by the brief vision. She was curious as to what had happened, but decided not to dwell on the incident.

Five miles later her vision turned to frightening reality when the car in front of her smashed into a pickup truck. Sheila had only a split second to maneuver before she, too, would slam into the pile-up.

Forewarned by her vision, however, Sheila instantly and automatically cut her steering wheel hard to the right. The two cars in the accident skidded to the left. The maneuver

Sheila made was the only path to safety. Sheila's car—and family—escaped by inches, unscathed. At the same moment she heard the terrifying sounds of several cars behind her crashing into the accident tangle.

What Sheila had experienced was a premonition received through Psychic Vision. At the time, Sheila knew nothing of the world of clairvoyance, and did not understand her uncontrolled Psychic Vision experience. Today she knows that everyone has two kinds of vision: normal physical vision—seeing with our physical eyes; and Psychic Vision—seeing with our "mind's eye" or "third eye."

This chapter will teach you how to develop your Psychic Vision. You will learn how to enter the world of clairvoyance and find your own third eye. You will learn to identify and interpret the different types of Psychic Vision. You will experience ways of using the screen of your mind's eye to visualize psychic information. And you will discover how your dreams relate to Psychic Vision.

In short, this chapter will raise the curtain for you on a whole new dimension of visual information. You will no longer be psychically blind, but will be able to see with your mind as well as your eyes. If you prove to be naturally strong in Psychic Vision, you will come to understand why you tend to think in pictures and why you so often need to "see" a decision before actually making it. Finally, this chapter will help you to deal effectively with the clairvoyant people in your life, and guide you in the skill of creating your own success through visualization.

Clairvoyance: The World of the Inner Eye

Through the ages Psychic Vision was usually referred to as clairvoyance, which means "clear seeing," since it allows you to see clearly beyond the reach of your eyes. Clairvoyance is that form of ESP which expresses itself as a picture, image, or visual impression. Traditionally, it is associated with receiving visual insights either through meditation, through dreams, or, as Sheila did, through a visual premonition.

Whether you realize it or not you have had numerous experiences with clairvoyance in your life, such as the time a sudden mental image of an old friend appeared to you, and then you got a phone call or letter from that person. When you visualize with your mind you are tapping your Psychic Vision, and the images that appear are clairvoyant impressions. Every time you dream or daydream, the subtle mental images also use the psychic inner eye. In effect, Psychic Vision is like having an internal television screen that displays information and pictures not available to your physical eyes. You may think these experiences are coincidences. I know they are your Psychic Vision at work.

Once you acknowledge that you *are* psychic, and that clairvoyance is not totally unfamiliar to you, the next step is to learn how to tap your Psychic Vision at will.

The Vision Psychic Reception Area

Metaphysical philosophers believed the seat of Psychic Vision was an area in the forehead. They called it the third eye. This forehead/third-eye region is in fact the Vision Psychic Reception Area. Many religions anoint or decorate that forehead area in baptismal or other blessing rituals. Many schools of meditation tell students to focus their thoughts there and visualize an image or scene.

Traditionally, the third eye was also thought to be linked with the pineal gland. Buried deep in the frontal center of the brain, the pineal is the most mysterious of the endocrine glands. Its function is not yet fully understood, but science has associated it with complex functions of light sensitivity

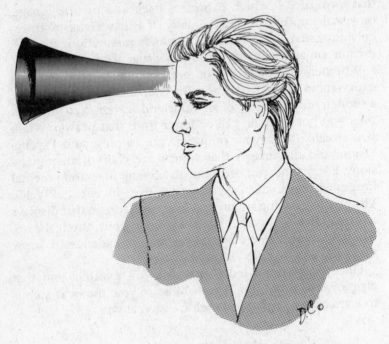

Figure #4   The Vision Psychic Reception Area

in both man and animals. An even more logical connector between the forehead region and Psychic Vision, however, is the frontal cortex. The final stages of visual interpretation take place in this front part of the brain that lies in back of the forehead. Locating the third eye in the forehead long seemed to be in direct contradiction of the presumed fact that visual information was processed in the occipital lobes at the back of the brain. But in computer images of the brain's electrical activity done by inventor Jesse Salbs for the PBS series "The Brain," it can be clearly seen that the final stages of interpreting and organizing visual impressions do in fact take place in the frontal lobes. Of particular interest are the patterns registered when you are dreaming. During the REM (rapid eye movement) portion of sleep—when dreams are most frequent—the brain shows a high incidence of frontal cortex activity but almost no activity in the rear occipital lobes. Dream images are seen with the mind rather than the eyes.

Psychic Vision works the same way. You receive images directly with the mind's eye. What has been missing in the metaphysical teachings about the third eye is how you can sense its exact location and know without a doubt where it is for you. Focusing in the forehead region is the best way to activate the third eye. With this knowledge you will be able to tap Psychic Vision on command, and discover the unfolding of your powers of clairvoyance and Aura Vision.

Remember that you have both physical and psychic vision. Over the years you have been trained to use your physical vision to the exclusion of your Psychic Vision. As a result, the latter skill has atrophied. You still have it, but it has to be reawakened. You need to start paying more attention to your Psychic Vision instead of looking only through the windows of your physical eyes.

Here is an easy way to prove that you do have both physical and psychic vision. Open and close your eyes. Notice how and where your attention shifts when you close your eyes. You will find that the moment you close your eyes your attention shifts upward. With your eyes closed, with the windows of your physical vision covered, all you have left is your Psychic Vision. As a result, your attention is naturally pulled upward toward that third-eye region. Try it a few times. Notice that upward attention-shift each time you close your eyes.

The following technique will help you to identify precisely your Psychic Reception Area for Clairvoyant Image Reception. It will show you how to locate the centers of your physical and psychic vision and open the gateway to the inner eye.

Locating Your Third Eye

1. Before pinpointing your exact Vision Psychic Reception Area location—your third eye—it is important to understand the foci or center points of both the physical and psychic vision fields. An awareness of how that center point shifts when you switch from physical to psychic vision is crucial to understanding and effectively using your Vision Psychic Reception Area.

2. Begin by finding the center point of your physical vision field. Relax and look straight ahead. While looking at the entire scene in front of you, feel where the center of your vision field is in relation to your face. For example, if a perfectly straight and level line were extended back toward you from the center of your field of vision, where would that line touch your face? Most people find that the center of their physical vision field lies between their eyes and about an inch below their eyebrows, approximately at the bridge of the nose.

3. Experiment to get the clear feeling of where your physical vision's center point is. If you are having difficulty, extend your arm, point a finger at yourself and with your eyes open gradually bring your finger closer and closer to you (keeping it in the center of your field of vision) until it touches your face. Do not stare at your finger. Look straight ahead and keep your finger in the center of what you see until it touches your face. This point is the center of your physical vision field.

4. Now find the center of your Psychic Vision field. Before proceeding, however, take a minute to sense fully the center of your physical vision field. Feel how you can identify this area and be aware of its existence. Now close your eyes. See if you notice any shift in your vision field or its center. Most people feel a slight but distinct upward shift, for when you close your eyes you will in most cases automatically switch from physical vision to Psychic Vision. With your eyes open you have both vision capabilities, but you usually ignore or are unaware of your Psychic Vision in favor of the physical vision you have been trained to use.

5. Open and close your eyes. See if you can feel the shift. Now, with your eyes closed, try to feel the center of whatever visual perception you have even if all you see is blackness. Most people find the center to be higher than their physical vision center—generally in an area of the forehead half an inch to an inch above the eyebrows. If you have difficulty feeling that center point keep your eyes closed and bring your finger toward yourself until you touch your face. Try to keep your finger in the center of whatever you are perceiving with your eyes closed; it does not matter what you see, even if it is total darkness; just stay in the center of it. Developing your awareness of this vision-field and center-point shift is the key to understanding and using the Vision Psychic Reception Area. By focusing your visual attention more in this area you will find it easier to receive psychic visual impressions.

6. With your eyes open, gently shift your focus of visual attention up to the Psychic Reception Area. See if you feel a greater awareness from or in this area of your visual field. Note your impressions and feelings, and compare them with your experience when you look with physical vision or focus on a different part of your vision field.

If you practice this technique with another person and his or her center points are different from yours, you are both right. Everyone has and feels a slightly different center point for both the physical and the psychic vision fields. The important thing is not the exact location of these center points, but the shift that occurs when you change from physical to psychic vision. Once you master the shift you will have on-command ability to experience both Clairvoyant Image Reception and Aura Vision.

Dreams Are Clairvoyant Experiences

Dream images are a form of Psychic Vision everyone has experienced. Although science cannot yet say for certain how or why we dream, it is a fact that in a dream you see without using your eyes. All dreaming uses the psychic screen of the mind's eye, whether the dream is nothing more than a random image, a mental review of the day's events, or a timely signal about the future. Frank's dream was a timely signal.

A pragmatic electrical engineer who could recall no previous psychic experiences, Frank had a dream one night of great vividness. He was driving his car over a railroad crossing when the lights and bells signaling an oncoming train started up and the crossing gates that blocked both lanes began descending behind and in front of him. Frank had to make a split-second decision whether to brake and back up, or accelerate and dash forward. In the dream Frank saw his car lurch forward and just make it under the crossing gates. Next day Frank's dream became a reality; he even remembered it as he approached a railroad crossing with gates long enough to block both lanes on both sides of the tracks. As his car started across, the barriers began to come down. Because of his dream Frank sped across without hesitation and made it through safely. When he looked in his rear-view mirror he saw a car immediately behind him. If Frank had tried to back up, he either would have been trapped on the tracks or been rear-ended.

Sometimes the message is so strong it repeats itself until fully received. Kathy Neal, a Free Soul instructor in Denver, had a striking clairvoyant experience with a series of dreams about a woman she did not know. In the first dream the woman spoke but gave no clue as to who she was or why she was in the dream. As the dream recurred over the next several nights the woman's face became clearer. Finally,

Kathy would have recognized it anywhere—and that, it seems, was the purpose of the repetitive dream.

Two weeks later, at a crowded meeting, Kathy saw that face. Because of the dream she introduced herself to the woman, and both felt an instant rapport. They have been close friends ever since. Through Psychic Vision Kathy was given an advance introduction to a woman who would be her special friend.

Keys to Dream Interpretation

The main difficulty most people have with clairvoyant dreams is how to interpret them accurately, for Psychic Vision is the most symbolic of the four psychic senses. That symbolism is especially apparent in the semiconscious state of dreaming. Balanced on the boundary between two dimensions, you have one foot in the psychic realm where the dream impressions are originating and the other in the physical world where you are trying to record and make sense of the message. As a result, many dream impressions tend to be more symbolic than literal. In either case, the first step is to shift your focus upward to your Vision Psychic Reception Area and review the dream with your "third eye." That can open the door to evaluating your dreams.

The second step is to decide whether the dream's images are to be taken literally, or as symbols of a deeper meaning. In general, the stronger the psychic message the more you will receive clear literal images. A literal dream will have a vivid forcefulness to it: The feelings and sounds of the dream will be strong, loud, and clear. Further, you yourself will be actively present in most literal dreams. You will see yourself in the dream rather than just seeing a scene. Both Frank's and Kathy's dreams are examples of literal dreams.

Symbolic dreams tend to be fuzzier. Since the psychic

message is not strong enough to generate a clear image, your mind substitutes symbols that represent the message trying to get through. Because of the lower psychic strength, the whole feel of the dream will be weaker. To interpret symbolic dreams you must first learn what your own symbols mean. For example, people often dream of someone dying, or of having a child. These common symbols indicate the "death" of an old state of consciousness, or the "birth" of a new phase of one's life.

Interpreting your own clairvoyant symbols is not as hard to do as it may sound. Remember that every psychic message simultaneously resonates on all four psychic frequencies. Thus you can use the other psychic senses to help you interpret the symbols in your clairvoyant images. If you are high in Psychic Feeling ask yourself, "What does the picture *feel* like it means?" If you are high in Psychic Intuition, follow your intuitive knowing and trust your first impression of what the image means. If you are high in the rational aspects of Psychic Hearing, let your logic help you unravel the symbol's meaning.

Belinda's dream offers a good example of a symbolic dream and how to interpret it. She had gone to bed one night still trying to decide about a career move: whether to stay in her Los Angeles job at a higher salary or take another position in Santa Barbara, ninety miles to the north, that would mean a temporary pay cut but greater job satisfaction. That night she dreamed of the rolling green hills and rugged coastlines of her childhood home in Ireland. But she did not see herself in the dream at all.

Belinda had grown so weary of the business rat race that at first she thought the dream literally meant she should go home to Ireland. Later she realized that the significant element in the dream was the feeling she had as she viewed its scenes. The green countryside and beautiful ocean still gave her the sense of inner serenity she remembered from her childhood. Intuitively she knew that the lack of such a peaceful environment was a major factor in her dissatisfaction with Los Angeles. It made logical sense that the dream was symbolically telling her to take the Santa Barbara position—that renewing her inner serenity was more important now than financial security.

When I met Belinda at one of my Southern California lectures, she had been in Santa Barbara for three months. After visiting with old friends in Los Angeles, she did not regret her decision. The quality of her life was vastly improved. To top it off, she had just gotten a raise that brought her salary to its former level.

Interpreting Your Own Dreams

The wonderful thing about dreams is that the psychic messages they carry are captured and encapsulated like mental crystals. You can go back and interpret any dream at any time. All you need to do is remember the dream, shift to your Vision Psychic Reception Area to rescan it, and tune in to your other psychic senses while you review the images. You now know how to do all of this. No longer need your dreams remain mysteries. Now you can use the world of clairvoyance to understand the psychic messages you receive during sleep. Practice with some of your recent dreams. Here is a review of the key steps to remember.

1. Bring to mind one or two recent but unclear dreams.

2. Shift your attention up to your Vision Psychic Reception Area and review one dream in your mind's eye.

3. As you do, note your feelings, intuitions, and understandings.

4. Write down your sense of the meanings of the images as you review them.

5. If you see several possible meanings, write them all

down. Then check your other psychic senses to determine which seems closer to the mark.

6. Let your psychic impressions lead you gradually to deeper and deeper levels of the dream's meaning. Explore all of its aspects and sidelights.

7. Continue this psychic scanning and reviewing process until you feel solid and complete about the interpretation you have worked out. At some point you will feel that click of certainty, of everything fitting. Stop there. Don't push for other meanings that are probably not present.

You can apply this simple but extremely effective process to any dream, whether recent, recurring, or a mystery from your past. The only limiting factor is how well you remember the dream. Because dreams occur during that twilight-zone boundary between physical and psychic realms, your memory of them can be fleeting if you don't capture and record them as soon as you awake. You don't need to write down the entire dream. Often just a list of keywords and phrases is enough to lock the dream into your memory for interpretation later. Trying to interpret a dream immediately upon waking will usually just put you to sleep again. Record the dream and interpret it later as part of your morning meditation, or do it that night as part of your review of the day.

The same process is just as effective for working with clairvoyant visions you may have when you are awake. These Psychic Vision daydreams are equally valid and frequently vitally important (as Sheila's story at the beginning of the chapter proves). Learn to be open to your inner vision twenty-four hours a day. Daytime clairvoyance is nothing more than the natural psychic use of your mind's eye. Once you know the Vision Psychic Reception Area you can look at life from two perspectives simultaneously. You can see the physical scene taking place in front of you and at the same time be aware of the psychic view behind it.

Psychic Vision or Imagination?

Skeptics argue that inner vision is nothing more than imagining. True, Psychic Vision and imagination do use the same inner screen of the mind's eye. But Psychic Vision is different from mere imagination. It is the use of the mind to receive images clairvoyantly rather than *generating* the images itself. For an analogy, consider the way VCRs work in combination with a television set. Think of the TV as the screen of your inner eye. When you are imagining, it is like using the VCR to create pictures on the television screen by inserting a tape of what you are imagining. When you are using clairvoyance, however, it is like having an antenna—a psychic receptor—which is gathering signals being broadcast around you and feeding them into the TV set. Both the antenna and the VCR use the same television screen to convey their images, but the source of the two pictures is quite different. The psychic antenna picks up signals that are beyond the scope of the imagination's videotape.

Exercising your imagination and practicing visualization does improve your ability to see psychically, however. The more you use either one, the clearer your mental pictures will be. In this way Psychic Vision and imagination are linked. If you think again about the TV-set analogy, you will see why practicing visualization techniques can aid the development of your clairvoyance. If you improve the picture by adjusting the color and contrast on a TV while playing a videotape through a VCR, reception will also be improved when you shift modes and operate the TV with the antenna. Similarly, the mental-focusing practice you get from imagining and visualizing will also improve the clarity of your psychic images when you want to receive clairvoyantly.

Don't Ignore Your Clairvoyance

Many people ignore the clairvoyant impressions they already are receiving. They think their mental pictures are only a reflection of their wandering mind, especially if the images they see are unrelated or symbolic (like colors, odd shapes, or scenes from old memories). While it is true, as we have said, that Psychic Vision is the most symbolic of all forms of ESP, don't make the mistake of thinking that the symbols are meaningless. Each clairvoyant picture carries a message.

To understand why Psychic Vision can be so symbolic, it helps to follow the process involved when you receive a clairvoyant image. Your conscious, thinking mind and brain are receiving signals on a frequency different from those of the world of the physical senses. When brain and mind attempt to translate those signals into terms you can understand, symbols are often the result. The old saying has it that one picture is worth a thousand words. Sometimes a simple string of picture symbols can carry reams of psychic information.

Frequently these symbols can be scenes from an earlier time in your life. In fact, symbols that spring from your visual memory are often more accurate and descriptive than abstract images. Our visual memory of an event or a situation contains a whole set of feelings, interactions, or warnings. As a result, it provides a much fuller meaning than a mere series of colors or shapes. And when the psychic message is strong or familiar, your clairvoyance can bypass the symbolism. In these cases the image you see is literal and clear. As the dream anecdotes showed, it can even carry exact information about the future. This wide spectrum of types of clairvoyance is the other major reason that many people miss the full potential of their Psychic Vision. Learn to recognize and use all four types of clairvoyance.

The Four Types of Clairvoyant Images

1. The Abstract Picture or Symbol is usually a color, color pattern, or figure. Because they are so abstract or symbolic, these images are often missed or ignored (even though we do see them unconsciously). People who do not think of themselves as psychic tend to disregard these abstractions, to consider them merely as daydreams or mental static. Once again we can make an analogy to a television set. Even if you are not paying attention to a TV set when it is on, images are still flashing across the screen. If someone asked you what was on the screen, you probably couldn't say—even though you knew *something* was there. You may be missing your clairvoyant images in much the same way, by not giving attention to them.

Let me give you a personal example. When I returned to the U.S. after five years overseas, I needed to buy a car. When I looked at new cars I saw in my mind's eye nothing but a blank screen; in one case, even worse, the image of a lemon. One day I passed a car-rental agency that was selling some of its used autombiles. My eyes were drawn to a Thunderbird that evidently was not for sale. When I closed my eyes I saw vivid green arrows and the characters *"4U."* I approached the manager and asked, "Can you sell me that car?" He said it hadn't yet been released for sale, as far as he knew. Moreover, he was using it as his personal car and didn't seem interested in finding out. I pestered the man for three days until he finally called his head office and was told the car had just been made available for sale. In spite of normal fears about used cars and the 12,000 miles it had been driven by who knows what kind of drivers, I bought it on the spot. My $5,000-lower-than-new-price car and I have been together now for more than 150,000 trouble-free miles.

2. The Visual Mental Memory clairvoyant image occurs when your brain translates psychic signals it is receiving into an image from your past that you can understand. The more extensive and experience-packed your life has been, the more visual images there are stored within your memory: places, pictures you have seen, particular events, and people. Clairvoyant image reception via visual memory basically makes use of an earlier image to help you interpret a current psychic message. The feelings, circumstances, or associations you have with the memory are the keys that unlock the psychic message.

Here is an illustration of how the message of a clairvoyant visual memory enhanced the professional career of my friend and fellow Visionary, John Hill. A Free Soul instructor in Colorado, John is one of the finest photographers of Rocky Mountain landscapes. He and his wife Judy feature art-quality prints of Colorado's scenic grandeur in their Aspen studio-gallery. Part of John's normal weekly routine is to visually sense what areas are most likely to yield an especially artistic photograph. He often gets ideas for new locations and un-usual camera angles by receiving a flash memory of an earlier picture that had unique characteristics.

Seeking a new place where he might find a stand of aspen trees turning a majestic gold, John saw in his mind's eye a picture of virgin woods that he had seen in a recent photographic magazine. He instantly knew he had to find a similarly protected enclave of aspens to make a perfect picture. Hiking up to the Rockies' Independence Pass, John saw dozens of scenes of aspen trees, but something kept urging him to climb farther up the mountainside. There, he knew, he would find the image he had seen in his mind. Walking miles farther than he normally would, John at last crested a rise and saw an exquisite grove of white aspens. Soft light filtering through their golden leaves gave the grove a glowing peacefulness John was able to capture on film.

The picture was so striking that Aspen Airlines not only used it on the cover of an issue of its in-flight magazine, but ran a feature story on John and Judy's studio. That picture has been one of John's best sellers. He has always been thankful he followed his Psychic Vision.

3. *The Literal Visual Image* is an actual visual perception. It involves refining your Psychic Vision to the point where you can translate the incoming signal into an exact image or scene. This is the most advanced form of clairvoyant image reception and usually requires either extensive practice or a natural gift for psychic visual ability. Kathy Neal—whom we met earlier in this chapter—is a natural clairvoyant. Fascinated by the idea of ESP even as a child, Kathy had her first dramatic experience with visual ESP in the fourth grade on Valentine's Day. The youngster who came closest to guessing the exact number of candy hearts in a jar would win the jar and its contents. It seemed reasonable to Kathy that she should be able to look at the jar and see a number that would be correct. Kathy felt she would just have fun and try it. Without forcing, she closed her eyes and saw the number 462. She wrote it down as her entry and, as you have probably guessed, it was exactly right. Psychic perception became a reality for Kathy that day.

4. *The Premonitional Vision,* or view into the future, can be received through any of the four psychic senses. With Psychic Vision, views arrive either as dreams or visual premonitions. (Frank's experience is an example of a dream premonition, whereas Sheila's is an example of a precognitive vision.) Over the years one of the best documented forms of this type of psychic experience has been the visual premonition people have of a loved one in trouble or approaching death. In these cases the urgency of the signal is so strong that even a novice receives the message clearly.

One woman recalled an experience she had three weeks before her husband's death. In a dream Lydia saw herself in bed with him. Slowly his eyes opened: *"Honey, I'm going to die soon,"* he said. The dream was so vivid that Lydia woke with a start, and leaned toward her husband to see if he was all right. As she looked at him her Psychic Vision took over again. For an instant she saw a skull's hollow visage superimposed on her husband's face. After a few seconds the vision cleared.

Lydia knew without doubt that their fifteen years together would soon be over. Rather than panic or become fearful, she used the vision to help her make the most of each moment they spent together in the days that followed. Several weeks later her husband died of a massive heart attack. Despite her grief, Lydia was able to let him go in peace, for in those final weeks she had had the chance to tell him how much she cherished their time together. Unlike so many people who suddenly lose a loved one, Lydia, thanks to her Psychic Vision, was allowed to say her last goodbyes.

Don't Be Afraid of Clairvoyance

Experiences like Lydia's are what make some people afraid of being psychic. "I don't want to know about bad things going to happen or loved ones going to die," they say. That view doesn't make sense to me. In my opinion, *any* advance warning you get can only help. Even if nothing can be done to prevent the loss of a loved one, a premonition can give you time to value that person, to voice your loving feelings. Most of the grief counseling I see revolves around trying to ease the surviving person's anguish at not having had time to express those feelings. When you have advance warning of a problem you can often take steps to avert it. At a minimum, being forewarned helps you to be better prepared. If clairvoyance can improve the quality of life by preventing problems or lessening their impact, fearing it simply isn't logical.

It makes sense to develop your Psychic Vision for use in all life situations. Even though many of the examples in this chapter are startling or extreme, Psychic Vision can be beneficial in small ways in your daily life. How helpful would it be to see the true nature of people you deal with each day? Think of similar countless opportunities in your daily routine when you could look up at that higher Psychic Vision screen to see behind the surface scene. Learning to use your clair- voyance in daily life also improves your ability to receive clearly more intense warnings and critical messages. Psychic Vision can be a practical part of your life, not merely a parlor game or source of amazement. You have already learned how to shift your vision upward to the third eye. Why ignore that extra window you have to the world?

Why You May Be Missing Your Clairvoyance

Some people fail to make full use of their clairvoyant abilities because they look for the wrong quality of image, expecting their impressions to be brilliant, intense pictures that block out everything else around them, including aware- ness of their physical senses. This is rarely the case at first. The key word with clairvoyance is *impression.* What impres- sion do you have? What picture do you see in your mind at the moment? No matter what type of image you receive (literal, symbolic, or visual mental memory) expect the quality of the image to be evanescent and tenuous at first. When you are beginning to open up to your clairvoyance, your visions will not be full-color spectaculars, but subtle impressions. Learn to capture those wisps of clairvoyance and expand upon them.

Realize, too, that people with different psychic strengths see different styles of clairvoyant images. Most striking in its difference is the form of Psychic Vision common to people high in Psychic Intuition. Prophetics tend to see rapid mental images, almost like flash pictures. If you are high in prophetic knowing, you may think you lack any Psychic Vision because you can't make your clairvoyant images last. They appear in an instant and then are gone. That is all right. It is natural for you to see psychically this way. Since Prophetics' strength is their quickness, you should never try to slow down your flash impressions. Trust your intuitive knowing of what the image was. If you need more information, simply reflash the picture or cycle your images.

People high in Psychic Feeling tend to see images that are fuzzy rather than crisp. What they see frequently resembles impressionist art. If you are high in Psychic Feeling do not try to sharpen your impressions; instead, sense what kind of feel the gentler colors and impressions have, and what kind of feelings they give you.

People high in Psychic Audience frequently do not see images at all. They simply understand the overall picture—how everything fits together. Their descriptions often sound as if they are explaining a diagram or blueprint of what they have seen.

Remember: Don't Try, Don't Force

Trying to force clairvoyance will not work. When you try to force the visual image, or overconcentrate on it, you drive your awareness down into your physical eyes. As a result, you often wind up seeing nothing more than the darkness behind your closed eyelids. Keep focusing your awareness upward toward the Vision Psychic Reception Area. Allow the impressions to come to you.

As with all forms of psychic sensitivity, you should look for an impression to reach you within the first five to ten seconds. If you feel you have not received one by then you have probably missed it, or forced a return to your physical vision. Relax and start over. This time look for a gentle impression, flash picture, or mental understanding.

The best approach to take when practicing clairvoyance is

to do it for fun, as a game or experiment. Take the pressure off by giving up any preconceived notions of what you *should* see. Relax and see what comes to you. The following technique will help you practice tuning in to your inner eye. If you do it properly, you will receive a clairvoyant image that will tell something about someone around you. Experience the technique as a way to begin opening this higher form of vision for yourself. Later, incorporate it into your routine by checking out at least one situation or person clairvoyantly each day.

Clairvoyant Image Reception

1. Relax, sit comfortably, and close your eyes. Feel your vision shift as your eyes close, and focus your awareness on the Psychic Reception Area for Psychic Vision. Rest a moment here and see what images and impressions you receive. Feel the heightened sense of awareness you have when you tune to this area.

2. Write down the names of five people you know. Close your eyes and, one by one, bring to mind a name from the list. Sense through your Vision Psychic Reception Area and see what images or impressions you receive as you focus on each individual. Note the feelings, knowings, and understandings that accompany each image.

3. Be open to receiving any of the four types of clairvoyant image. If you get a pure symbol or color, note it. If a visual memory flashes to mind, note its feelings and circumstances. If you see a literal scene, get a feel for whether you are viewing a current event or seeing a premonition.

4. Do not try to analyze the impressions while you are receiving them. Simply record them and move to the next name on the list. This will help you stay in a psychic flow.

5. When you have finished all five, review your notes and analyze the images you received as your Psychic Vision sensed the vibration of each individual. What can your images tell you about that person, or about how to deal with him or her?

Note: If you have time and want to practice this technique further, or if you feel you will be less biased in receiving, write the names of five other people you know on slips of paper. Turn the slips over and mix them so you do not know which name is on which slip. Number them 1 through 5, and one by one hold each slip (with name hidden) in your hand. Close your eyes and see what visual impressions you receive. Record your impressions on a list numbered 1 through 5. After you finish, match the numbers to the individuals to see what impressions you received for each person. If possible, get in touch with them to find out if your images correlate either with their state of mind at the time, or with some event or activity affecting their life.

Still another way to practice Clairvoyant Image Reception is to get a symbol for *your* day. Sense a key image, or picture impression, that serves as a guide to behavior that will make your day successful. Hold yourself and that thought in mind and see what impression you receive. One morning when I was working on Clairvoyant Image Reception I got a picture in my mind of a charging bull. I interpreted it as a symbol to be unstoppably assertive that day. A few hours later I had the chance to apply that message: Through persistence and assertiveness I convinced two skeptical radio program producers to have me as a guest on their shows. The next day I received the image of a meditating figure and of a timepiece showing two o'clock. As a result I took time out at 2 P.M. for an additional meditation. When my phone rang at 2:30 I was calm and prepared for the unexpected interview with the *Washington Post* that followed.

Try to get a key image for yourself for today. Then focus on receiving an impression of a key image for tomorrow, for the next week, and for the month. Do not try to analyze while you are receiving. Just relax, note your impression, and interpret it after you finish and open your eyes. Record your impressions. What do they mean to you? Do they give you any insight? How easy was it to receive them? This technique can be an important practical aid in your daily life.

Personality Characteristics of the Psychic Visionary

Men and women who have Psychic Vision as the most natural of their extrasensory abilities tend to live their physical and psychic life from a visual perspective. This is what we in Free Soul mean by being a Visionary. Such a person experiences life as one vivid mental image after another. Whether planning a meal or one's life work, the ability to see the entire picture is his or her most important reference point and greatest strength.

Visionaries must have an inner picture; without it they feel lost. In contrast, the Feeler and the Prophetic do not require an inner picture plan. Feelers are willing to "go with the flow"; as long as things feel comfortable they will enjoy the moment without much concern for the future. Prophetics know the plan will come to them in time, so they continue to rely on their instincts to adapt moment to moment. Visionaries can't function that way. They must have their inner picture to feel solid. One could say that Visionaries without their pictures are like Prophetics stripped of their intuition or Feelers forced to stay in a discomforting environment. While a Visionary person needs not only to see the total picture but to see it with all its connections, the Audient is more concerned with understanding how the current situation can be explained. Just as the Audient wants to understand *why,* the Visionary wants to see *how* things will fit together. Without that complete view the Visionary is as unmovable as the Audient is without his understanding.

I'm sure it is clear by now that for persons strong in Psychic Vision, the first step to success is to form a complete inner picture. Taking time to visualize and plan gives them inner stability, a firm foundation from which they can go forward with confidence. Given time, Visionaries can always see the most productive life course and build a comprehensive plan that will integrate all its elements. They are the masters of advance planning.

For Visionaries, time spent visualizing and daydreaming is a necessity. This visual ruminating is where they get their best ideas and set the direction for their life. Visualization for them is more than just wishful thinking. It is the psychic projection of a road map they can follow to success.

Visionaries Need to See Things Physically as Well

For a Visionary, seeing is essential to wise decision-making. That is why physical vision helps trigger deeper levels of Psychic Vision. Remember my experience with buying the used car? Physically looking at the car drew me to it, and then triggered the symbolic psychic vision that confirmed its rightness for me.

If you are high in Psychic Vision, physically looking at the objects or location involved in a decision will provide additional reassurance. Whereas the Prophetic just knows if something is right, the Visionary must see it to know that. The Audient can listen to someone on the phone and get a sense of the person; the Visionary will want to meet him or her in person. The Feeler will want to get close or even touch people to get a better feel for them; the Visionary will want to stand back to have a fuller view. Of course that same desire to see means that the Visionary likes plenty of windows in his home, or scenic views when she travels, and as many lights on as possible. How can you see what's important to you if all the lights aren't on?

A Visionary's Love Affair with Light

An amusing instance of this classic Visionary trait occurred to me during one of my first intimate encounters. It had been a delightful evening of good conversation and shared rapport, almost like meeting an old lover after a long separation. One thing led to another, and before long I was moments away from unveiling what to me was a whole new world of visual stimulation. Suddenly my partner turned cold and backed away. "What's wrong?" I asked. "Do you realize every light in this room is on?" she asked. In my mind I said, "Of course. This is a memorable moment, and I want to see every beautiful detail of it."

To me, having as many lights on as possible made perfect sense. After all, a Visionary needs to see what he or she is doing to be most effective, and this was one time I didn't want to make any mistakes. My partner, who was higher in Psychic Feeling, shared neither my visual needs nor my concerns. After a quick mental readjustment my actual response was something like, "Sorry, I didn't notice." I may be a Visionary, but I'm not stupid. Some lights were turned off in a hurry, but the essential ones stayed on.

In any kind of intimate relationship Visionaries have to have light and visual stimulation. To Feelers, touch, embrace, and physical closeness are essential. For Audients, talking and being listened to are key elements. People high in Psychic Intuition seem to be best at adapting intuitively to the needs of their partner.

The bedroom is not the only place Visionaries like to have

light. They want it everywhere, sometimes to the consternation of others. Visionaries frequently leave lights on when they leave a room because they want them already on when they come back. Bob and Pam were students of mine in Baltimore. Bob was high in Psychic Vision and always left lights on in their home. Pam, who was higher in Psychic Feeling and didn't need them, constantly trailed Bob to turn them off. One night when Pam returned home she said, "Why is every light in the house on?" "Because Bob and I were teaching the class tonight," I said. "How else would two Visionaries have it?"

Bob and Pam had been at odds about the lights for months. Now they knew the reason lay in their different psychic strengths. They settled the matter by agreeing that Bob could leave the lights on in his study (even when he wasn't there) if he remembered to turn them off in the other rooms.

Don't Change the Visionary's Picture

Another distinctive characteristic of Visionaries is their initial resistance to change. Remember, Visionaries have an internal picture of how they expect everything to be. That inner picture is their security and reference point. When someone wants to change that picture, or presents a new idea (no matter how good) that complicates the plan, they will resist strongly. Their whole aura will scream, "Don't change my picture!" This can make Visionaries seem rigid and inflexible. If you force an immediate answer about a picture change, you will always get a resounding "No!"

If you must suggest a change to a Visionary, the secret of success is to introduce the idea calmly and give the person time to reshape his or her inner image. When an idea is introduced without pressure, Visionaries can always eventually visualize a way to work the change into the total plan. For this reason, give the Visionary time to think.

If you are high in Psychic Vision, sleeping on ideas is an excellent policy. Allow yourself time to reshape your perspective. Don't say "No!" immediately. Rather, say, "Let me think about that and get back to you tomorrow." You will usually come up with an even better master plan that incorporates the new idea.

To Please a Visionary . . .

Since Visionaries like everything involved with the world of seeing, take them to a movie or a museum; watch television together; buy them picture books. At a theater or sporting event, get seats with the broadest view; put them next to the window when traveling, and at the end of the table where they can see everyone at once. And remember to never, never turn the lights off on them.

In the next chapter you will experience another facet of Psychic Vision—the aura. Being able to see auras is the gateway to a new dimension of awareness. It is a psychic gift waiting for you to open it.

Clairvoyance—Psychic Vision

ADVANTAGES

Best for integrating the four psychic senses into a plan of action
Best for sensing all aspects of someone's aura
Best psychic sense for spotting problems

Best psychic sense for proving ESP to yourself (seeing is believing)
Most detailed of the psychic senses

DISADVANTAGES

Most symbolic of the four psychic senses
Can be hard to distinguish from imagination or daydreaming
One of the slower psychic senses

People High in Psychic Vision

STRENGTHS

Excellent at seeing how to integrate all factors into a master plan
Are good at visual-spatial problems (packing, furniture arrangement, and the like)
Can naturally see when something is not right, and know what is wrong with it
Can visualize situations, problems, and solutions in their mind
Have an excellent sense of time, plan well with calendars
Have an excellent sense of direction, can get anywhere with a map
Are outstanding color coordinators, keep the world visually interesting

WEAKNESSES

Can be rigid and inflexible (not wanting their picture changed)
Frequently will not act until they have the whole picture

Are the world's best worriers (they visualize everything that could go wrong)

Can tend toward perfectionism ("it's not right unless the picture is perfect")

Can be highly self-critical (seeing and emphasizing their faults more than strengths)

• 6 •

Sensing the Aura— Psychic Body Language

AURA. It's a word we all have heard. Some of us use it in our everyday lives when we seek to describe a special person or object. "The painting has a magical aura," we say, or "I like the aura of that room," or "She has a bright aura." The word pops up in the names of boutiques, and there is even a magazine called *Aura.* It would seem that the idea of an aura has captured our imagination.

But is it an imagined essence, a mythical attribute, a superstition? Or does it actually exist?

The aura has been described metaphysically as the radiation of a person's spiritual energy through the body, along with the effects of thoughts and feelings being projected at them. I think of the aura as a psychic X-ray. When properly interpreted, it can reveal a person's mood, intentions, health, feelings, and motives. Sensing auras can serve as an advanced way to read the signals of a person's body language—a way that offers extended insight into his or her personality.

I am often challenged about my belief in auras. People ask, "As a scientist, how can you believe in them?" I reply quite simply, "Seeing is believing." I know that auras exist because I see them, and I use the information I get from them every day of my life. After you have learned the keys and techniques in this chapter, *you too* will be able to see auras.

Aura Vision Saves Money and Prevents Problems

Frequently, the information I receive from sensing an aura is the basis for my decision-making about people, places, events, and even objects. For example, my wife and I recently bought a new house—but only after I used my Aura Vision to avert two potential future disasters. The house I wanted to buy was being sold by the owner-builder. Bob was a warm, enthusiastic man with a friendly face. He told me in great detail about the structure of the house, and how agreeable the neighbors were who owned the adjacent vacant lot. As the house was on the edge of a hill with little yard space, I was concerned about where our two children could safely play. Bob said the neighbor would not only let my youngsters play on their vacant lot, but would also allow me to park our second car there. As Bob told me that cheering news, I watched his aura begin to ripple—a sure sign that his promises were not fully accurate.

Bob also told me how much extra care he had put into the construction of the house. This time I watched his aura go from strong and solid to incomplete (lacking a strip down the middle). This indicated to me that there was something missing in the construction that even Bob might not consciously be aware of. I resolved to check into both auric inconsistencies. First I called the man who owned the vacant lot. I found him to be anything but the cooperative person Bob had described. When I told him that Bob said I would be able to park in the vacant lot, the man said he had never given anyone permission to park there. He was upset that Bob had done so without consulting him. The idea of children playing there was definitely out of the question, he said. Moreover, the man believed that a retaining wall Bob had built as part of the house up for sale was actually on his side of the property line. If a survey proved it, the man said he would sue to have it taken down.

Next I wanted to check the construction. I hired a structural engineer to inspect the house. He reported that though in general the house was well built, a key interconnecting brace was missing, making a main roof-support beam unsafe and potentially deadly. As a result of my investigations Bob agreed to correct the structural flaw at his expense, and to ensure in the contract that if the retaining wall did indeed encroach on the adjacent property, he would pay the costs of its removal and appropriate restoration. As it turned out, a survey did show the wall to be on the other man's property. Bob paid an out-of-court settlement to let the wall remain undisturbed and the house undamaged.

Explaining the Aura Scientifically

In the world of subatomic physics today, science is often stranger than fiction. Science has proven the existence of the neutrino—a particle that has no observable mass, no electric charge, nor any other physical properties, and is thought to be capable of traveling at the speed of light and passing through any barrier. Nuclear physicists almost routinely produce antimatter particles and send them hurtling around accelerator rings. Each year they discover strange new forces and hitherto unknown particles.

With all this in mind, believing in the existence of an auric energy field around the body is really not so farfetched. In fact, an electromagnetic process called Kirlian photography has produced images that resemble what many psychics see as auras. Particularly striking is the "phantom leaf" effect, where an auric image of a whole leaf appears in the photograph even though the tip of the leaf was cut off just before the Kirlian photograph was taken.

A full explanation of what causes the aura or what energies make it up still eludes us. Some people call it the body's spiritual energy field. Others think of it primarily as electromagnetic radiation. What we do know is that millions of electric signals course through our nerves each second, and that each impulse produces a constantly changing mini magnetic field. I have no doubt that in the years ahead science will find that the aura is a complex combination of electromagnetic radiation and as-yet-unknown energies.

Until then you will have to let your personal experience be your gateway to the world of auras. No matter what your psychic strengths are, you too can see, feel, know, or understand the auras of people, things, and places. Auras can give you your best insights when choosing a doctor, a new automobile, a baby-sitter, a spouse, or—as in my case—a home to live in.

Since Psychic Vision is the ESP channel most commonly associated with the aura, let's start your learning process with how to see auras. Even if you don't think you are gifted in Psychic Vision, read the following section carefully. There is an exciting visual surprise waiting for you. Later in this chapter you will learn how to use Psychic Feeling, Psychic Hearing, and Psychic Intuition to sense someone's aura as easily and effectively as with Psychic Vision.

Three Keys to Successful Aura Vision

• Auras must be viewed with your inner eye. You cannot see an aura with your physical eyes; you see a person's body with your physical eyes. If you try to see an aura with your physical vision alone, you will fail. Most people cannot see auras because they try to "force" seeing them through their physical eyes. When seeing an aura, you are using Psychic Vision superimposed on the physical image you see with your physical eyes. Together they give you the combined body and aura picture.

• Do not try to see an aura by staring. When you stare, your awareness becomes locked at the level of your physical eyes. Look past the person. Look over his or her shoulder, or above and around his or her head. Relax your eyes. Let them go out of focus. This automatically helps you shift your awareness up to your Vision Psychic Reception Area.

Take a moment to experience this for yourself. Notice that when you stare at something or someone, your awareness is pulled away from your Psychic Vision center and locked at the level of your physical eyes. Compare where your awareness is to what you experienced when you located your Vision Psychic Reception Area in the previous chapter. Now try looking past an object: Instead of looking *at* it, look *through* it and at the wall behind it. Or instead of staring at a person, look past him and just keep his image in the foreground. Notice that when you do this, your attention automatically shifts upward. Notice that when you look past that person or object, your awareness seems to be focused in the brow area you identified as your Vision Psychic Reception Area.

• Use gentle control to stay focused at that third-eye area. The shift will take place automatically when you relax your physical eyes. Remain conscious of maintaining the higher focus. If you slip into staring or are distracted, reshift your attention back up to that Vision Psychic Reception Area. Realize that you can be in command of turning on your Psychic Vision.

The real secret of learning to see an aura is not to force or overconcentrate. As with all things psychic, the harder you try, the less likely you are to succeed. Learn to focus your awareness and gently guide it to where you want it to be. Staying tuned to your Vision Psychic Reception Area requires a lighter touch, a subtler awareness.

An excellent physical example of this lighter awareness can be experienced with peripheral vision (side vision). If you try to force a clearer image of something in your peripheral field, the natural tendency is to shift automatically into staring, and for your head and eyes to turn to bring the fovea (center of the retina) to bear. If, instead, you relax and allow your attention to focus at the side of your visual field, you can see just as clearly without turning or forcing. Try it. Notice the difference in feeling between the forced concentration of staring straight ahead, and the gentle focused awareness of *attending* to your peripheral vision. This more gentle form of focused awareness is the secret to psychic experiencing.

Seeing the Light Ten Years Later

Elaine Gibbs, now a Free Soul instructor in Fort Worth, Texas, is not particularly strong in Psychic Vision. Elaine studied in the spiritual and psychic fields for ten years, and all of her training convinced her that everyone should be able to see auras. Yet she had never succeeded in seeing one. Elaine didn't know it, but for ten years she had been trying *too* hard. She consoled herself by deciding she didn't really need to see auras; she had other ways of sensing a person's psychic energies.

When at last she entered the Free Soul program and tried my simple methods, Elaine's feelings changed. She understood the practical benefits of seeing auras, and trained herself to stop staring, stop forcing, and start relaxing. With that, after ten years of failure, she saw an aura.

In one of our first classes she made that upward shift to her Vision Psychic Reception Area and looked past a person. "I let my eyes go out of focus and became aware of the back of his head and there it was, an aura," she recalls. "I was amazed at how easy it was."

Elaine's example is a dramatic one. It will not take you ten years to develop your Psychic Vision or begin to see auras. You can learn to see an aura today if you apply the principles and techniques in this chapter. Remember not to force. Be patient with yourself; you are developing a new skill. Furthermore, it is important not to try to analyze what you are seeing while you are seeing it. Until you are proficient at Aura Vision, an immediate attempt to analyze what you are seeing will weaken and frustrate your Psychic Vision. This is not to say that the thinking mind is unimportant. But it will compete for your attention and limit your initial Aura Vision effectiveness. Receive first; after the experience is complete, analyze the results.

Avoid the Afterimage Trap

Some psychics who say they are teaching Aura Vision are actually only showing you how to see an afterimage. An afterimage is the physical effect of the bleaching of retinal pigment in your eyes. Staring at a bright color for a prolonged period of time bleaches out certain pigments in the retina. Then, when your eyes shift or when you view a white background, you see white minus the color that has been bleached out (what is commonly called the complementary color). For example, red and green are complementary colors; so are blue and orange, and yellow and purple. If you stare with your physical eyes at a person wearing a bright yellow outfit, and then look at a white wall or shift your eyes slightly, you will see a purple, violet, or blue (depending on the shade of yellow) afterimage. Conversely, if you stare at someone wearing purple, you will see a yellow afterimage. The same is true of the red-and-green combination.

It's important to know the complementary colors, and what an afterimage is, so you don't think you are seeing an aura when in fact you are still physically staring and merely seeing an afterimage color. People who have been taught, either intentionally or inadvertently, to see afterimages, and who think they are seeing an aura, are actually locking themselves deeper into physical vision. True Aura Vision will become more difficult for them because they have taught themselves to stare rather than relax.

You can avoid this problem if you start to practice seeing auras around people who are wearing white or light-colored clothing, and if you learn the complementary colors. Thus, if you see a yellow pattern around someone wearing red, that is an aura, because yellow is not red's complementary color. If you see a red color around someone wearing blue, you will know you are perceiving an aspect of the aura rather than an afterimage, because red and blue are not complementary colors.

Opening Your Own Aura Vision

Follow this step-by-step process to begin opening your Aura Vision. If you are sitting where you can see people, try it now. If not, study the guidelines and practice them later. In either case, remember not to force. Do not overconcentrate. Focus. Allow yourself to experience. Remember where your Vision Psychic Reception Area is, and use it to combine simultaneously your psychic and physical visual fields.

1. Go where you can observe people—preferably people who are sitting still in front of a light background—or ask a volunteer to assist you.

2. Face the subject from about ten to twenty feet away. Become aware of your Vision Psychic Reception Area. Without looking at the person, relax and focus your awareness in the third-eye region of your forehead. Leave your eyes open, but shift your attention upward to your Psychic Vision.

3. When you feel in tune with your Vision Psychic Reception Area, observe the person in front of you. Let your eyes rest on him or her while you focus on your Vision Psychic Reception Area. If you do this properly, you will feel as if you are looking more from the level of your forehead than from the level of your eyes. Do not look directly at the person, but rather beyond or just slightly over his or her head. This naturally shifts your awareness upward to the third-eye area.

4. You will begin to see a one- to three-inch band of light or glow around the outline of the body. The effect will be strongest in the head and shoulder areas. This is how most people begin to see the aura: as a halo of light around the other person. The more you relax, and the more your subject relaxes, the wider and more distinct this halo will grow. Eventually you will see colors and colored areas within this field, as well as above the head and in front of the body. *Note:* As your Aura Vision is fairly new, the colors probably will be transparent, evanescent, easy to see through. Do not expect to see vivid or solid colors that completely obscure your view of the individual. Look more for a subtle color impression.

5. Try this with several people so that you view the auras of different subjects. Notice how some persons' auras are wider than others, and how different color patterns appear around each subject. The width or intensity of the aura can give you a good idea of a person's level of relaxation as well

as the vitality of his or her energy field. The various colors can serve as clues to the other person's basic characteristics and personality traits.

This technique is designed to introduce you to the vast field of Aura Vision, and to help you see that first halo or transparent energy field around a person. As you relax more fully and become comfortable with the process, you will see more vivid colors and sharper impressions.

Practice: Essential for Aura Vision Success

Not long ago a hostile young man belligerently asked me, "Why don't I see auras automatically yet?" I inquired how many times he had practiced Aura Vision during the last week. "None," he said. Then I asked how often he had practiced during the last month. Again he replied, "None." My final response was, "And it surprises you that you don't see auras automatically?"

Improving your Aura Vision is entirely up to you. The more you practice, the easier it will get. You can make use of various home and work situations to improve your ability. Any time or place you can observe fairly motionless people, and are able to relax and flow with your impressions, you can practice viewing auras.

Learning your Vision Psychic Reception Area is the catalyst that unlocks the door to seeing auras. You are the one who must push that door fully open. The more you practice, the more you will gain experience with the many different characteristics you can see in an aura. Don't feel, incidentally, that you have to see color to be able to use Aura Vision. Even in the early stages, when you see only an initial outline of an aura, you can use Aura Vision to tell you more about the people you deal with.

The Two Dimensions of Aura Imagery

Aura imagery has two dimensions: color and shape. Most people think only of seeing color when they speak of seeing an aura. As you learned from my home-buying story, color is not always the most important aspect of Aura Vision. It is equally important to be able to recognize the depth of the aura's boundary, its texture, shape, and intensity. Notice if the aura seems tighter around certain areas of the body. Notice if the boundary is smooth or ragged. Assess the quality of the aura's strength and illumination.

These aspects can tell you how relaxed a person is, whether he or she is able to be receptive, and whether he or she is mentally focused. For instance, the more relaxed a person is, the wider the aura. If the aura is tight around the body it usually means that the person is under tension and pressure. The calmer the individual, the wider the aura.

If a person is in a meditative or reflective state of mind, the boundary of the aura softens, becomes more blurred. Day-dreaming creates the same effect. If, on the other hand, the person is focusing creatively on work, he or she will tend to have a relaxed, wide aura but with a clear, sharp boundary. It will also be radiant around the head.

You can tell if a person is listening to you or not by checking to see if his or her aura boundary is crisp and sharp. If the boundary is blurred and fuzzy, chances are you are being tuned out. When the aura ripples or seems to shimmer, it's time to double-check what the person is saying.

All of us want to be more effective communicators. Studying the aura of a person you are about to approach can provide additional insight into how best to reach that person. If his or her aura is bright and tight, his or her mind will be active and quick. In that case, to be successful present your ideas quickly and be succinctly assertive. If the aura is relaxed and wide around the head, you will know the person is in a reflective or pensive frame of mind. Don't approach this person forcefully; be prepared to settle for a more gradual discussion of your project.

Practice what you have just learned. For an interesting test, see how well you can match the state of mind with the correct aura shape by drawing a line to connect one with the other:

State of Mind	Aura Shape
Relaxed, calm	Fuzzy, blurred boundary
Tension, pressure	Rippling or shimmering
Meditative, daydreaming	Wide, expansive
Listening, focused	Sharp, distinct boundary around head
Lying or exaggerating	Tight around body

How well have you done? A relaxed, calm state of mind will have a wide, expansive aura. Tension and pressure will show an aura that is tight around the body. A meditative daydreamer will have a fuzzy, blurred aura boundary. If a person is listening and focused, the aura around his or her head will have a sharp, distinct boundary. A lying or exaggerating person will have a rippling, shimmering aura.

Basic Aura Vision Warning Signs

Even without seeing colors in the aura, you can use your aura impressions to alert you to potential problems. Here are a few basic aura warning signs that can be helpful in everyday life. You can sense these impressions visually or as a feeling, a knowing, or even a mental understanding. By paying attention to them you can avoid serious errors in judgment. At a minimum, they can lead you to investigate further.

THE DOCTOR

1. His or her aura is weak and dim. Would you feel he is rested enough to give you competent care?
2. His aura is drifting away from you rather than being directed toward you. Do you think he is fully focused on your case?
3. His aura ripples and shimmers slightly. Is it possible he is not telling you everything about your diagnosis or the side effects of your medication?

THE BABY-SITTER

1. The aura seems overwide, flimsy, and shimmering. The sitter tells you he or she can handle any problems. Do you believe it?
2. The aura boundary is fuzzy and erratic. Is it possible that the sitter is using drugs?
3. The aura tightens when the children approach. Does the sitter really like children?

A PARTNER/CO-WORKER

1. The aura changes noticeably when he or she speaks to different people. Is this person sincere? Or have you just discovered the office phony?
2. The aura is withdrawn and shifts away when you try to focus on it. Is there something that person is deliberately not telling you?
3. The aura seems to extend through and beyond you. Will this person walk over you to get what he or she wants?

A LOVER

1. The aura is ragged, scattered, and uneven at the boundaries. Did your partner have a hard day? Does he or she need to unwind for a while? Is this the best time for love?

2. The aura seems to reach out for you. Should you be talking business or bed?

3. The boundary of the aura is solid, hard, and inflexible. Is this a headache that's liable not to go away?

4. The aura is firm but softens as you spend time together. Is this the time to be slow but sure?

Sense the auras of people you meet during the next week. See if you can notice some of the characteristics and aura effects I've described. Remember that feeling, understanding, or intuitively knowing other people is as psychically valid as seeing the aura itself. So be sure to note *all* your impressions, not just your Psychic Vision ones.

Color Interpretation in Aura Vision

Once you have learned to relax and see the basic aura boundary, you can continue to open your third eye and notice the colors you sense or see. Color adds a whole new dimension to the information you can gather from your Aura Vision. The following list is designed to be a general guide to help you interpret the meaning of the colors and color patterns you may see in an aura. Just as each of you has your own set of past memories and associations, each of you also has your own unique color codes and keys for the way you perceive the energy field around other individuals. Remember, too, that you will always be viewing the other person's aura through your own aura. This guide can serve as a starting point for developing your own interpretation system. It describes the common characteristics, energies, or vibrations that can stimulate the appearance of various colors in the aura.

RED: Energy, vitality, strength, hard work, or strong emotion; dark reds can signify tension, frustration, anger, hatred, or malevolence; pinks can indicate joy or enthusiasm; basic red is also the color most associated with Psychic Audience.

ORANGE: Courage, or being faced with a challenge.

YELLOW: Open, communicative, having insight, or visually perceptive; the color most associated with Psychic Vision.

GREEN: Growth, teaching, a new beginning, change, regeneration, healing, or the new beginning after an illness is nearly over.

BLUE: Sensitivity to feelings, caring, peaceful harmony, or healing (the blending or adding of energy during an illness); blue can indicate needing or receiving healing energy, whereas green indicates the self-generation of healing effects and new growth; blue is also the color most closely associated with Psychic Feeling.

PURPLE AND/OR VIOLET: Spirituality, deep thought, or future orientation; the colors most closely associated with Psychic Intuition and prophecy.

BROWN: Practical, down-to-earth, earthy, or sensual.

GRAY: Businesslike, organized, in a strictly business mode, or busy.

BLACK: Pressure, tension, injury, or dysfunction; black around the body usually indicates outside pressures or tensions; over the body it can mean physical injury or disease.

WHITE: Purity, innocence, clarity of motives, newness, or balanced integration of all energies.

SILVER: Idealistic, trustworthy, nobly principled, sincere.

GOLD: Regal, of high value; wisdom and mastery, or spiritual abundance.

Now that you know the predominant characteristics reflected by the major colors, you can put the colors together to create the total picture of what a person may be feeling. The key for doing this most effectively is to notice around what area of the body the color appears.

• Colors above or around the head and shoulders usually reflect an individual's state of consciousness.

• If the color is around but well away from the body, it usually relates to aspects of the person's life or environment.

• If the color is directly over the body, it tends to relate to the person's health or physical energy.

For example, light green around the head indicates a growing desire for change. Black around the body indicates pressure at work or in the environment. A slight darkening in the aura over the body shows increasing physical tension not yet bad enough to be intolerable. If you view a person whose aura meets that description, you will know you are looking at someone with a growing desire for change because of pressure and tension in the environment. His or her physical energy level may still be acceptable because frustration has not reached an intolerable level.

Test Your Color Interpretation Skills

See how well you can match the following personality types or emotional frames of mind with the aura color patterns that describe it:

AURA COLOR		WHICH ONE FITS IT?
1. Strong but dark reds	A.	*Sensual Sam/Sue* In the mood or can definitely be talked into it

2. **Warm browns and yellows**

    B. *Philosophical Phil/ Phyllis*
Constantly questing and exploring new ideas about the future

3. **Gentle but deep blues and yellows**

    C. *Angry Al/Alice*
Intense and under pressure; stay out of the way

4. **Bright, vivid greens and silvers**

    D. *Moving-Forward Marc/ Marge*
Changing and growing but well motivated and totally trustworthy

5. **Pulsing purples and golds**

    E. *Empathetic Irv/Irma*
Feels for all people and is frequently oversensitive to others' troubles

Answer key: 1C, 2A, 3E, 4D, 5B.

There is no limit to the number and variety of ways you can use Aura Vision and its advanced versions to sense people, situations, or environments. For me, Aura Vision has become a natural skill I can turn on at any time. I use it to get a deeper view of the person or situation at hand. When I add this to the information I get through my physical senses, I am able to see a broad picture.

Aura Vision Rescues an Interview

Once in Washington, D.C., I was about to begin what I thought would be a difficult interview on a major television program. The host was known to be less than receptive to the topic of ESP, and from watching the show the day before, I knew he had an aggressive way of asking questions.

As I waited for the program to begin I switched on my Aura Vision and focused on the host. Since I was scheduled to be the first guest, I looked to see what his aura could tell me about how best to handle the interview. Checking first to see what the host's psychic strengths might be, I noticed at once the strong red colors around the sides of his head. These usually appear on people who are high in Psychic Hearing. From the personality characteristics associated with Audient people, I knew the way to reach this man was to help him understand. Providing him—and thus his listeners—with clear explanations would be the key to making the interview a success.

As the director signaled, "On the air," there was a fascinating change in the host's aura. The opening camera shot had the host stand facing the camera while the Smithsonian String Quartet (scheduled to be guests on the show later) played in the background. I saw the man's aura dim in front and almost bend around backward as he was distracted by the music behind him. The effect of this auric disruption was immediately apparent. The host couldn't read his opening words smoothly from the Teleprompter. He stuttered and stammered, muffing one word after another. His aura was shifted so strongly behind him that his forward concentration was shaken.

As he sat down to begin talking to me, the interviewer said repeatedly how embarrassed he was at blowing his opening lines. I explained what his aura had told me about his psychic strengths, and what I had seen happen to it as the quartet began playing. He was fascinated by my explanation. Instead of attacking me, he helped me to do an outstanding television interview. Later he said, "That's the first time anyone ever explained something about ESP that made sense to me."

Sensing the Aura with Psychic Feeling

If you are highly gifted in Psychic Feeling, you may be more likely to *feel* an aura than actually see it. At least, your feelings will help you interpret what you are beginning to see with Psychic Vision. Sensing the aura through Psychic Feeling is just as valid as seeing it through Psychic Vision. Since the aura is an energy field that exists beyond the physical senses, whatever psychic ability best enables you to reach beyond the physical should be your preferred method for sensing auras. Moreover, impressions you feel are easier to interpret than colors you see.

To tap aura awareness through Psychic Feeling, sense what you feel about the person or object being viewed as you look for the aura. You need not necessarily see specific colors or aura aspects. Simply let your attention center on the area where the aura should be. Ask yourself, "What does the aura boundary feel like? Wide? Tight? What feelings do I get when I look at the area where the aura should be? What color do I feel is around the person's head?" For Feelers, aura-sensing can be as natural as following their feelings. Feelers often sense in their own aura, or in their body, the characteristics present in the aura of the other person. That way, Feelers can sense someone's aura without ever seeing it.

Anna Marie Nowak is a registered nurse and a Free Soul instructor in Philadelphia, Pennsylvania. In her work at an institute for the mentally handicapped, she dealt with autistic children, among them sixteen-year-old Rory. Like all autistic children, Rory is withdrawn; even when he does interact with the staff, he never speaks. Obviously this made it difficult to diagnose or treat any injury or illness he had. Rory grew agitated when something hurt him or when he felt ill, and through his gestures and an examination the nurses usually could tell what was wrong.

One day, however, Rory was more agitated than usual.

Flailing and gesturing frantically, he could not be calmed. Yet no one, and no type of physical examination, could find anything wrong with him. Anna Marie tried a different approach. She tuned to her psychic sensitivities, trying to sense Rory's energy. Her first impression, through Psychic Feeling, told her that the boy's aura was weak; that its protective outer layer had dissolved; and that he was being bombarded by the intense psychic and emotional vibrations that occur in even the best of institutions. Anna Marie knew instinctively that he needed an energy boost—a psychic "jump start," if you will—to recharge and expand his aura and give him the energy buffer he lacked.

Placing her hands at two key centers on his head, Anna Marie let energy flow through her to Rory. This psychic therapeutic touch helped him to recharge and smoothed his battered vibrations. By this time she had a crowd of onlookers from the infirmary staff, because Rory had never before let anyone touch him for more than a few seconds.

As Rory rocked, Anna Marie kept her hands gently on his head and continued to channel energy to him. Within a few minutes his movements slowed, then stopped. With a peaceful sigh the youth gently rested his head on Anna Marie's side. He had no need for medical treatment. All he had needed was a spiritual and psychic energy boost. Because Anna Marie could sense Rory's aura with Psychic Feeling, she was able to offer the appropriate holistic treatment.

Knowing the Aura with Psychic Intuition

Prophetically gifted people can depend on their intuition to enhance their Aura Vision with their instant knowings. The key for Prophetics is to trust that intuition, to believe in what they get even if it is just a flash, even if they didn't really "see" it at all. Prophetics' psychic impressions can come and go in an instant. When viewing an aura, then, what they see can be just as fleeting—a sudden insight, a brief burst of color. Rather than try to make the color last, they should ask, "What is my first impression about what I saw? What do I know intuitively?" Knowing the aura via Psychic Intuition can be so rapid that Prophetics may get impressions even before they start to look.

When Prophetics trust and follow their inner knowings, they are invariably right. Why bother to slow down that instant accuracy? It doesn't make sense to force a knowing into a picture, and then have to interpret the picture. If you are high in Psychic Intuition, trust and act on your knowing.

For example, Free Soul instructor Terry Padilla, a therapist at Washington County Mental Health Center in Montpelier, Vermont, was working late to organize patient files in her office when Brenda, a fellow therapist and friend, asked if she could come in and sit down for a while. Terry immediately sensed something wrong, and when Brenda remained silent Terry switched into psychic sensing mode. Scanning told her that Brenda's aura was weak; the area over the heart, particularly, gave the impression of a gaping emotional wound. Terry neither saw nor directly felt anything; she just knew Brenda had been hurt.

Terry told Brenda what she sensed, and suggested that Brenda visualize placing a bandage or an energy patch over that area until she could get herself back together. That was all the prompting Brenda needed, and her story poured out. Her competency had been attacked in front of other colleagues by a fellow worker, someone Brenda considered a friend. She felt violated. "How can I face any of them again?" she asked. "Maybe I should just quit my job."

At Terry's continued urging, Brenda visualized her whole body wrapped in an energy bandage that would desensitize her to the emotional pain. Almost immediately Brenda felt stronger and able to go about her work. Terry benefited, too. The experience proved to her that she could trust what she intuitively sensed about an aura even if she did not actually see it. Since then Terry has improved her aura-sensing abilities. It is now a standard part of her screening of clients and patients.

Understanding the Aura

For Audient people, the key to aura-sensing is analysis and understanding. Audients "figure things out," or "try to understand what makes you tick" so automatically that they seldom realize when part of their analytic impressions is psychic. The logic of their psychic sensing is hard to distinguish from their normal mental functioning. Thus they may not even know when they are reading a person's aura.

Instead of images and pictures, Audients psychically receive words and phrases about a person's aura that enable them to understand the personality traits that person is radiating. This inner awareness is so close to Audients' normal mental dialogue that they think they are merely analyzing the person.

There is one distinction, however. An Audient's impressions tend to be stronger when the other person is talking. Since hearing is the physical sense most closely linked to clairaudience, listening to the person talk helps the Audient tune in to the aura. And since Audients can listen "between the lines," they should note the impressions and understandings that come to them apart from the actual words. Impressions of a voice quality, for example, can carry psychic information. Were the words friendly, but the tone harsh or rigid? Was the guarantee made, but lacking in firmness?

When Carol Swersky, a Free Soul instructor and self-development counselor in Aspen, Colorado, was giving a seminar on psychic development, the topic of auras came up. "What do you do if you can't see auras?" someone asked. In reply,

Carol described the four psychic senses and explained how the aura could be sensed by any of them. To demonstrate she singled out a woman in the audience: "When I look at you and think about your aura," Carol said, "I sense the words pink and green." With another woman Carol reported that she heard the words green and blue-green.

Both women were astounded. The first woman said she had just redecorated her home in pink and green. Using her Psychic Hearing's mental understanding aspect, Carol told the woman those colors indicated a need for healing time— green for physical healing, pink for spiritual renewal. "That's exactly why I'm in Aspen," the woman said.

The second woman provided even further confirmation. She had recently consulted a clairvoyant who saw the same two colors in her aura that Carol had "heard." There was another interesting development: This second woman had never seen an aura but frequently heard words when trying to see one. She always ignored the words, but now knew she could sense auras in that way.

Make Aura-Sensing a Part of Your Life

If you use what you learned in this chapter, you know that you—that everyone—can have a form of Aura Vision no matter which psychic ability is your strength. Success may not be automatic at first. It will take work and practice, but the rewards are invaluable. The psychic information you glean will give you instant feedback on everything you do. Practice scanning the auras of the people in your life and prove your ability to yourself. Make sensing the aura even more real to you by learning to scan your own aura as well. You take a look at everything else before you go out: your hair, your clothes. Why not check your aura? Either with a mirror, or with your feeling, knowing, and understanding, sense your aura and determine if it needs adjusting. Since the aura is keyed to your state of consciousness it takes only a thought to smooth or expand it. You can mold its boundary into any shape you wish by holding that thought in mind.

In the next chapter we'll explore more deeply the connection between body and mind and how you can use it to take greater command of your inner physical being. You will learn how to control your body with your mind and how to promote Inner Healing.

• 7 •

Self-Healing—
Latest Breakthroughs in
Biofeedback

A YEAR AGO I set out with a group of friends, all colleagues in Free Soul, on a raft trip through the Grand Canyon. Along with a dozen other vacationers, we were looking forward to the excitement of running some of the Colorado River's roughest rapids, and to the challenge of the ten-mile hike out of the canyon.

Not surprisingly, many of the people in both groups wondered how they would stand up to the physical demands of the trip. If anything, our group of Free Soul men and women had more to be concerned about. Several were in their late forties and fifties; a few were overweight; three had difficulty breathing due to asthma and chronic bronchitis, and one woman had lost part of a lung; two people had knee problems. All in all, not exactly the kind of folks you'd expect to come out of the canyon without a lot of aches and pains and complaints. Yet when, a few days later, we all reached the canyon's South Rim, our group was in high spirits and fine physical fettle while our fellow voyagers were mentally and physically exhausted.

The difference was not in our bodies but in our minds; not in our physical capacities but in our mental abilities. For each person in our Free Soul group knew something that those in the other group did not: how to use those mental abilities to help our bodies cope with the trip's physical demands.

After the first day's rafting we were exhilarated, yet at the same time relaxed and at peace. Using stress-reduction techniques, we had ridden the rapids calmly and even assisted another rafting boat that had flipped over. The other group traveling with us was fatigued and tense. On the second day we were greeted with one of the furious sudden summer storms that occasionally rage at the bottom of the canyon. Within minutes the temperature dropped 40 degrees. The blistering sun gave way to pouring rain, roaring winds, and even a bombardment of hail. The rain and wind were so severe that our motorized rafts had to pull to the side of the river and wait as visibility closed to a mere few yards.

How the two groups dealt with the storm was another indication of the difference between us. The people in the other raft huddled under the seats, shivering in the cold. The chilling 48-degree river spray from the earlier rapids we had passed through added to their discomfort. Our group tuned in mentally, tightened the boundaries of our auras, and readjusted our internal thermostats to stay warm. Instead of suffering in discomfort, we climbed a nearby hundred-foot cliff and meditated on top while watching the grandeur of the storm sweep through the canyon.

The trek out of the canyon really emphasized the contrast between the two groups. Even though most of the Free Soulers were not hikers, they had learned how to channel energy and use biofeedback techniques to sustain their bodies and help muscles recharge. I mentally sent strength and support to an injured knee with each step. The woman who had lost part of one lung mentally kept her body calm to compensate. All of us made it to the top and were exhilarated by the climb. When a friend arrived to pick us up, we were having an ice cream party and enjoying the oneness we had shared with nature. The other group? Most of them were collapsed in the lobby of Bright Angel Lodge. One man, a surgeon, said, "We'll never do this again!" Instead of conquering the Grand Canyon, they were beaten by it.

Which group do you want to belong to—those who enjoy the challenges of life and triumph over its stresses, or those who fall victim to life's rigors? There is no reason you cannot belong to the former group.

Once you learn the skills of inner healing that will be explained to you in this chapter, a new adventure in mental freedom over physical limitations will open for you. We in the Western World now know what yogis in the East have known for centuries: that with advanced biofeedback techniques the mind can enhance *any* bodily function, even those once thought to be beyond conscious control.

You can tap this new mental dimension and use it for everything from stress reduction to enhanced vitality and health. This chapter will give you keys that unlock the biofeedback abilities of your mind. You will learn how to quickly cleanse your body of the negative physical and psychological effects of stress. You will be able to lower your blood pressure and regulate your pulse. You will learn how to travel within your own body and direct healing to any part of it. In short, you will achieve a new level of mental mastery over your physical being. Once you learn to use your mind to assist your body, physical challenges will be less threatening, stressful situations will be handled calmly, and the body's self-healing abilities will be at your disposal.

Preventing the Body's Damaging Stress Reflexes

The first step in learning inner healing is to prevent the way your body can involuntarily harm you. Stress and stored tension are probably the two main contributors to physical and mental disease. We all face stress. How you deal with it is the key to whether your life is an exciting quest that you command or a constant test to which you must submit.

As the pressures of daily life increase, our ability to handle the stress they generate has deteriorated. These additional pressures also lead to increased demands on our time and cut into the period of relaxation our body needs to unwind and recharge. The problem is further compounded when people take their tensions to bed with them and wreak havoc with their normal sleep cycles. When you add to this a lack of training in how to induce relaxation consciously, the result can be devastating.

Science has only recently begun to document the effects of mind-body control for stress reduction, but already the results are striking. Biofeedback techniques are now used for everything from lowering high blood pressure to reducing chronic pain to enhancing athletic performance. At the heart of this mind-body revolution is what Dr. Herbert Benson of Harvard Medical School calls "the relaxation response."

Dr. Benson has been studying the effects of mind on the body for over twenty years. Not long ago he served as an expert advisor on a public television network program called *Discover: The World of Science.* One segment of the program, called "Minding the Body," took place in the meditation room of a lamasery near Tibet. Monks entered the room and soaked sheets in buckets of ice water. Sitting in the lotus position, they draped the wet, freezing sheets over their naked bodies.

Then, using an advanced form of yoga called Tumo Yoga, the monks consciously began to raise their skin temperature. Within minutes the sheets began to dry; the increased heat from the monks' bodies started them steaming in the frigid air.

Dr. Benson electronically monitored the monks' physical reactions while they meditated. His instruments showed increases in skin temperature of as much as 15 degrees in an environment where it should actually decline. Tibetan magic? An illusion? Clearly not. The monks had learned to use mind-body biofeedback to control consciously what is normally an involuntary biological response.

This dramatic proof of biofeedback once again confirmed the validity of Dr. Benson's early theories and experiments. He had further found that a person under stress, or a person who perceives himself under stress, will show an increase in blood pressure, heart rate, and the level of stress hormones in the blood. If this reaction occurs too often or goes on too long, it can cause or aggravate a host of physical ailments such as hypertension, ulcers, colitis, and heart disease. Dr. Benson reasoned that if stress and the body's reaction to stress hormones are triggered mentally, a *reverse response* could also be stimulated by the mind to lessen their negative effects. That reverse option is what he called the relaxation response.

The term *relaxation response* seems to me to emphasize the physiology of stress reduction rather than *your part* in it. For that reason we in Free Soul prefer to use the term *Auto-Relaxation* as a way of emphasizing the fact that it is a mental process, and that you yourself are in complete command of generating it.

With Auto-Relaxation the body calms itself. Blood pressure drops, heart and breathing rates drop. The flow of blood through the muscles stabilizes, and there is a growing sense of tranquility. These immediate effects have long-term benefits as well. Individuals who regularly induce Auto-Relaxation show a decreased sensitivity to one of the body's major stress hormones. As a result, when under stress they do not tense up as quickly; their bodies automatically react more calmly to the alarm signals.

Mind over Body: Hypertension Relief

Sophia suffered from hypertension all her life—until this year. She dreaded her annual physical exam. Her family has a history of high blood pressure and Sophia's frequently rose over a dangerously high 200/140. Each visit to her doctor brought the same lecture about watching her diet and reducing stress. Each time she was warned of the potential serious illnesses her hypertension could cause. Sophia became so nervous about having her blood pressure taken that just the thought of it sent her pressure higher.

But this year things were different. Sophia, who recently took the Free Soul course, practiced daily our breakthrough methods for quickly triggering Auto-Relaxation. This year her blood pressure was 140/90, its lowest in twenty years. The doctor was amazed; Sophia was thrilled. Now, instead of constant doses of expensive drugs, she uses her mind to help control her hypertension.

A Key to Auto-Relaxation

Hypertensives in hospital outpatient groups, and others with chronic pain, currently are taught to use a twenty-minute meditation process to elicit Auto-Relaxation. Most of us don't have the time to spend twenty minutes meditating on calmness, or even longer to chant a mantra as recommended by some Eastern spiritual organizations. Those of you with families or young children are probably thankful to get even ten minutes of personal time in your day. What is needed is a quick and effective way of triggering Auto-Relaxation.

I have found such a way and call it the Relaxation Breath Pattern. It is your key to rapid stress reduction and is the first step in learning mind-body control.

Breathing is the optimum gateway for learning mind-body control because it is connected to both the voluntary and the involuntary nervous systems. Normally, your breathing is regulated automatically. The autonomic nervous system senses the physiological conditions in your body and adjusts the depth and rate of your breathing accordingly. When you are under stress, your breathing automatically shortens and speeds up. When you are relaxed and at ease, your breathing deepens and slows down.

Breathing can be used to trigger Auto-Relaxation because, although it is directly linked to the body's physiology, it can also be controlled voluntarily. By consciously assuming and maintaining a breathing pattern associated with relaxation, you can induce that physiological state in your body. The secret is to find the rate and depth of breathing that *your* body associates with relaxation. Once you learn your personal Relaxation Breath Pattern you can go to it instantly and begin to induce Auto-Relaxation and stress reduction in a matter of moments.

Finding Your Personal Relaxation Breath Pattern

The Relaxation Breath Pattern is that depth and rate of breathing that is most calming for you physically. It is different for each person, varying with one's size, weight, and lung capacity. Moreover, most people who use breathing methods to relax frequently do the wrong thing. They usually go too far. They take breaths that are too deep or too slow and actually tense up again. If you have tried controlled yoga breathing (only one or two breaths per minute), you know that until you build up your lung capacity, the technique is difficult and at first tenses rather than relaxes.

The secret to identifying your Relaxation Breath Pattern is to find that point where taking even a fractionally slower or deeper breath begins to feel uncomfortable. You can locate that point simply by becoming aware of your breathing, by gradually slowing and deepening it until you reach a point where to go any further requires effort. Once you reach your Relaxation Breath Pattern, mentally focus on inhaling calmness and exhaling tensions. Within a few minutes you will feel stress draining away. Your body will enter Auto-Relaxation and you will experience a sense of peace and well-being. Let's try it. But before you begin note how you feel inside. How unstressed and calm do you feel? Compare this with the state of relaxation you achieve after using your Relaxation Breath Pattern.

1. Comfortably sit or recline. In meditation or relaxation techniques there is no magic to any particular posture or position—the choice is yours as long as it satisfies the following three requirements: (a) it is comfortable, so that you are not distracted by physical sensations of pain or discomfort; (b) it is not sleep-inducing (so comfortable that you consistently can't keep from falling asleep in that position); and (c) it is one that you can or do associate with relaxation or meditation.

2. Once you are comfortable, become aware of your breathing. Notice the frequency and the depth of your breathing. Gradually increase the depth of your breaths while at the same time slowing down your rate of breathing. Do this at your own pace and to a point where you are breathing at what *you* feel is the most relaxing and calming pattern for you—where to take even a fractionally deeper or slower breath would begin to feel uncomfortable. Stop there. This is your personal Relaxation Breath Pattern.

Note: There is no required manner for breathing (for example, through nose or mouth). Find the way that is most comfortable for you. Many people prefer to breathe in through the nose and out through the mouth. Also, you may keep your eyes open or closed.

3. Once you are comfortably maintaining your Relaxation

Breath Pattern, begin to focus mentally on relaxing with each breath. With each inhalation focus on breathing with greater calmness and peace. Visualize and feel relaxation flowing into you each time you breathe in. With each exhalation feel yourself blowing out the pressures and stresses of the day, and know that tension is draining from your body. Breathe in calmness and breathe out anything that stands in the way of maximum relaxation.

4. Maintain this focused breathing for 5 to 10 more breaths. Mentally command your entire body to relax and unwind. Hold in mind a time when you were completely at peace. As you breathe with your unique Relaxation Breath Pattern, feel that same peaceful calm flow through every fiber of your being.

5. After several minutes note how you feel. Compare your inner sense of calmness with how you felt before you began.

The more you use this simple technique the easier it will become to trigger Auto-Relaxation. Each time you follow the process described above it will be easier for you to recognize your unique Relaxation Breath Pattern. Gradually you will be able to lock into your mind the specific rate and depth of breathing that triggers Auto-Relaxation. Eventually you will need only a few seconds to find and slip into it. Moreover, each time you perform the technique your body will increasingly come to associate relaxation with that specific breath pattern. Before long just one or two minutes of breathing with your Relaxation Breath Pattern will lower your pulse, reduce your blood pressure, and release the negative effects of stress.

Because this is such a quick and simple method for triggering Auto-Relaxation you can use it anywhere and at any time. Practice a few minutes of relaxation breathing before an important meeting or interview, and you will find you can deal with those situations calmly and be in control of them. Similarly, if you are suddenly faced with a stressful situation, or feel tensions building, try using your Relaxation Breath Pattern. You will feel tightness and anxiety melting away. Eventually you won't even need to close your eyes to do the exercise. As a result, you will be able to use your Relaxation Breath Pattern to relieve stress when you are driving and find yourself in a traffic jam; or you can use it right in front of people who are trying to pressure you.

Learning your personal Relaxation Breath Pattern is a dynamic key for taking conscious control of stress reduction. Most important, once you learn it, the mere thought of that rate and style of breathing stimulates Auto-Relaxation. You do not have to do twice-daily half-hour meditations, chant mantras, or seclude yourself in order to achieve deep relaxation. You have learned a skill that is usable in all situations. You have learned how to achieve inner calm in a quick and practical way.

Mind over Emergencies

Bob and Paula, Free Soul graduates in northern Arizona, were joyfully awaiting the arrival of their first child when Paula's water broke two and a half months prematurely. The life of their unborn child suddenly was at risk in a race against time. Bob knew he needed to keep calm and steady, especially since the nearest hospital was thirty miles away over icy mountain roads. Bob used his Relaxation Breath Pattern to trigger Auto-Relaxation while he drove at top speed around slippery curves and along snowy straightaways.

More stress awaited Bob and Paula when they arrived at the hospital. Their doctor was away on vacation, and his backup physician couldn't be reached. Stage two of their ordeal would involve an hour's plane ride to Phoenix, the closest neonatal intensive care center. As Paula felt labor contractions begin she, too, used her Relaxation Breath

Pattern to calm her body. In Phoenix, still more stress: an unfamiliar hospital and doctors whom the couple had never met. The natural childbirth classes they had attended were useless now. The baby was starting to show signs of distress, and the doctors decided to perform an emergency cesarean delivery.

Bob and Paula had the same blood type, and with the threat of AIDS from tainted blood in his mind, Bob wanted to donate a pint of blood that could be used during Paula's surgery. He was told it would be possible only if his blood pressure was within an acceptable range. Resuming his Relaxation Breath Pattern, Bob focused on easing his pulse and lowering his blood pressure. After registering a near-perfect 130/85 despite the stress he had experienced, Bob was allowed to donate the blood.

Thanks to his controlled demeanor, Bob got permission to join Paula in the operating room. Things were not going well there. The spinal anesthetic wasn't taking properly; Paula still had sensation on one side of her body. The surgeons felt it was unsafe to wait any longer. With Bob coaching her, Paula again used her Relaxation Breath Pattern, this time to help reduce pain. She focused on calmness and detachment, the cesarean proceeded, and eventually the full effects of the spinal took hold. Bob and Paula's thirty-week, 2½-pound baby made it into the world safely. The child, fully recovered from the effects of prematurity, is now developmentally more than a year ahead of most babies his age.

Learning to Be Master of Your Body

Just as Bob and Paula used mental control to assist their bodies, you, too, can master this form of biofeedback. Once you have learned how to use your Relaxation Breath Pattern to trigger Auto-Relaxation, the next step to inner healing is learning to control your body's physical functioning.

Are you one of those who think of mind-body control as vague, mystical, and beyond your ability to experience? Or do you view it as a new form of scientific biofeedback equally unattainable by you because it requires costly and complex equipment? Neither view is correct. Mind-body control is possible for everyone. It requires neither mystical nor mechanical assistance. Controlling the body with the mind is now fully accepted scientifically as a method for the conscious direction of involuntary body functions. Whether you call it yoga or biofeedback, all you need to succeed is the desire to learn, a willingness to experiment, and the patience and discipline to practice. All three of these prerequisites are available to you.

In fact, you have been practicing mind-body control all your life. For years you have mentally controlled the actions of your voluntary muscles, physical senses, and overall coordination. It is worth remembering that no matter how ordinary or how natural it seems to direct the body's voluntary nervous system, it is no less a scientific marvel. You take it for granted only because you have done it successfully for years. I emphasize this point to help you realize that mind-body control is not totally new for you. The more advanced forms of yoga and biofeedback are merely the next step. They involve the conscious control of the normally involuntary or subconscious body functions and systems. While this is less familiar to you, it is only an extension of skills that you *do* possess and can learn to expand: those of *directing, influencing, and coordinating the wiring of your body.*

Almost everything that comprises our body is affected and reached by the electrical wiring that we call the nervous system. Even amid the many wonders of the body, the nervous system stands out as truly amazing. The enormous number of nerve cells and their vast interconnections throughout the body make the nervous system the most complex and extensive wiring framework known to science. The number of possible connections between nerve cells in the brain alone is 1,000 million million million. That is more than the number of atoms in the known universe. It is as if any one nerve cell can speak to any other nerve cell anywhere in the body. This means you have the wiring connections to order or influence any physical action or effect you desire. All that remains is to learn *how*.

The Two Nervous Systems

Your body has two different and independent nerve networks: the voluntary, or motor coordination system, and the involuntary, or autonomic nervous system. Both have almost infinite connections and cross-connections within the central nervous system of the brain and spinal cord. Why do we have two separate but equally important networks?

• The *voluntary nervous system* primarily controls the action and coordination of the skeletal muscles of the body. Conscious control of this system gives us a high degree of mastery over our environment. It makes possible physical movement, the manipulation of objects, and consciously directed actions in the world around us.

• The *involuntary or autonomic nervous system* is equally vital. It constantly but subconsciously controls and regulates body organs and their functions. This assures smoothly responsive operation of the body's internal physiology, and frees us from having to think of those functions that require continuous regulation to sustain life—blood circulation, respiration, metabolism, and so on.

The work of the involuntary nervous system has become so automatic, however, that our ability to override it temporarily has atrophied. The nerve connections for doing so still exist, however, and that atrophy can be reversed. You can learn to influence and enhance temporarily any of the body's automatically regulated functions. Studies show that active mental involvement can boost the body's natural health and healing mechanisms. Your success in self-healing is linked directly to learning mind-body control.

Unlearning Old Barriers to Self-Healing

To relearn the lost skill of conscious control of the body's autonomic functions you need first to unlearn old habits. Your primary experience with controlling your body has been with directing the voluntary nervous system and your skeletal muscles. For this, concentration is the key. As a result, you are used to concentrating, to forcing, to trying, when you are mentally directing your body. *These are precisely the wrong approaches for successful mental control of involuntary functions.*

The voluntary system is basically a network of dormant transmission wires waiting to be activated. The more you concentrate your thoughts, the more wires you activate and the better your fine motor control. This is not true for the autonomic nervous system. It is structured to function on its own. Its network is already working in continuous closed loops. To influence it and insert an override signal, a new form of thinking is required—a subtler and gentler touch. Forcing only throws you into activating the voluntary network and produces muscle tension. Relaxation, rather than concentration, is the key to achieving maximum success with mind-body control.

• Triggering Auto-Relaxation is the *first of three steps* for accessing self-healing skills. Because you now know how to do that with your Relaxation Breath Pattern, you are already one-third of the way to learning mastery of your body.

• *The second step* is to channel your awareness gently, to guide it and allow it to travel in the direction you choose. Because the nerve connections that control your autonomic nervous system are separate from those you are familiar with, you need to explore new ways for lightly focusing your inner mental awareness. This light touch is what gives you access to influencing the involuntary nervous system.

• *The third step* is to focus your awareness *in* the area you want to affect. Remember what I shared in Chapter 1 about how focusing my attention in the heart helped me to lower my pulse quickly far below my previous best? Letting your thoughts flow to the desired area and gently holding your attention within it are the keys to this third step. Don't force or concentrate. Instead of keeping your focus in the head area, let your consciousness flow to the desired location and be there mentally. You can practice this projected form of consciousness by taking your own "inner voyage" into the body.

The Inner Voyage: Sensing Your Body

Some years ago a Hollywood studio made a film called *Fantastic Voyage,* based on a book by science-fiction writer Isaac Asimov. It told the story of an ultraminiaturized "submarine" that was inserted into the bloodstream of an important scientist. The task of the similarly ultraminiaturized experts manning the vessel was to navigate the bloodstream, reach the scientist's damaged brain, and repair a blockage there.

In a sense—and certainly with less risk—you can make your own "fantastic voyage" into your body. That inner voyage is a body-sensing technique that forms the basis for physical self-knowledge and self-healing.

You will ride the nerve fibers to every part of your body; they are your highways to inner adventure and discovery. And once you are able to focus your awareness within any area of your body, you can go on to affect its functioning.

Do not force while learning the following technique. Let

your awareness channel down to the part of your body you want to visit. Let your attention be there from within. You don't have to see a particular image or feel a specific texture. Simply note your impressions as your awareness makes its inner voyage.

1. Close your eyes and briefly unwind, using your Relaxation Breath Pattern.

2. Feel a sense of yourself, your awareness, and feel in command of directing it.

3. Gently guide your whole being and attention downward into the body, and travel to one of your bones. Think of the bone and let your awareness flow down the nerves to be there. Sense the bone's strength and hardness. Feel the support it gives to the whole body. See if you can sense the activity going on inside the marrow.

4. Follow along the skeleton, traveling from one bone to the next, exploring as many different bones as you like. From a bone, move your awareness to a muscle. Sense its characteristics, its contracting and working ability. Extend your explorations and travel to several different muscles and muscle groups.

5. From a muscle let your awareness flow into a blood vessel. Continue traveling by riding the pipelines of the circulatory system to any part or organ of your body. As you do, note the feelings, images, and sensations unique to each.

6. Gently return your awareness to the center of your forehead. When you feel ready, open your eyes. Review your travels in your mind, recall the sensations and characteristics that go with each area and system you visited.

You have just traveled within your body. In your journey you have learned to extend your consciousness to any cell, tissue, or area. You can now focus your awareness on and within any part you want to affect with mind-body control. All that remains is to put these three steps—triggering Auto-

Relaxation, gentle mental focusing, and locational awareness—to a specific use.

Mind over Pulse: Learning Heart Control

Controlling your heart rate is a good way to begin practicing mind-body control because it is easily measured. All you
need is a watch that counts the seconds and the ability to
take your own pulse, either at the neck (on either side of
your throat/windpipe) or at the wrist. Although the throat
pulse is stronger and more easily detectable, I recommend
taking the wrist pulse because you can touch it with less
physical disruption. Hold one hand palm up. With the other
hand reach across your upturned wrist. About three-quarters
of the way across (just below the base of the thumb of your
upturned hand), press down with your middle two fingers.
Between the tendons and the bone you can feel the pulsing
artery that runs to the hand.

Before you begin, practice measuring your heart rate by
taking your resting pulse. Sitting down, count the number of
pulse beats you feel in 30 seconds. Multiply by 2 and you
have your normal resting pulse. Use it as the standard to see
how well you do raising and lowering your heart rate. First
try increasing your pulse. Here are some keys:

• Close your eyes and picture yourself involved in stren-
uous physical activity. As you do, feel your heart beating
faster and faster.

• Continue to visualize that intense physical activity and
take a brief "inner voyage" to the heart area. See and feel
your heart from within and mentally stimulate it to speed up
its pace to meet the demands of your visualized activity.

• Keep this up for a few moments, adding any other
visualizations you desire. When you feel you have increased

your heart rate, slowly open your eyes and take your pulse for 30 seconds. Multiply by 2 and compare the result with your beginning rate. An average increase of 2 to 5 beats per minute for this initial attempt is good. Anything more is better. How did you do?

We began with raising your pulse because it is usually easier to accomplish; since you are probably sitting as you read this, your pulse was already fairly low. Next, work on lowering your pulse.

• Begin by using your Relaxation Breath Pattern. Gradually breathe deeper and more slowly. As you do, sense your whole body starting to relax.

• Close your eyes and visualize your body going into a deep resting state almost like hibernation. Send to each cell a "thought order" to reduce its activity to a minimum.

• Again journey inward to the area of the heart, maintaining the image and sense of deep relaxation. Feel your heart contracting and pumping, and consciously will it to beat more slowly. As you sense your body going into that deep relaxation, visualize and feel the heart relaxing and slowing as well.

• Continue this for a few more moments, adding any other calming thoughts that are meaningful for you. When you feel maximally relaxed, slowly open your eyes and take your pulse for 30 seconds. Multiply this number by 2 and compare it both with your resting and increased pulse rates. A decrease of 2 to 5 beats per minute from the resting rate is average for this initial experience.

Heart rate is one of the easiest and most readily measurable autonomic functions you can affect with mind-body control. This first attempt to use the "inner voyage" technique allows you to experience, perhaps for the first time, your ability to mentally control aspects of the body that are normally beyond your reach. The more you practice, the easier it becomes.

Understanding the Body's
Self-Healing Mechanisms

Exploring the marvels of the human body is one of today's great scientific frontiers. The immune system, the brain, the world of DNA and the genes, all still hold many secrets. What we do know, however, unequivocally points to the potential for using the mind to help promote health. Every location of the body can be reached by existing nerve connections. Every cell has within its chromosomes the template for complete human regeneration. And it has now been proven that your state of mind directly affects your immune system.

Twenty years ago mind-body healing assistance was scoffed at; today many cancer patients are taught to use visualization to attack their tumors. A video game called "Killer T-Cell" has been developed to help children with cancer maintain a positive attitude, a sense that they can take part in the battle against their illness. To play the game, which is quite similar to Pac-Man, the youngsters guide an on-screen "T-Cell" to gobble up symbols that represent attacking cancer cells. A direct link between the level of T-cells (the immune system's main fighter against disease) in the blood and a good mental attitude has also been scientifically established.

Dr. Bernie S. Siegel of Yale University Medical School is one of many prominent physicians and psychologists who are exploring the connection between a positive, directed state of mind and an enhanced immune system. If you feel good about yourself, your T-cell level rises. If you feel depressed about your situation, it drops and you become more vulnerable. A positive frame of mind working to combat illness changes the body's internal chemistry. The resulting healing is not miraculous or spontaneous; it is logical, scientific, and self-initiated.

None of this is deisgned to encourage you to abandon traditional medicine or to fail to consult your physician when necessary. My aim is to show you ways to assist their efforts or, through prevention, to not need them in the first place. The more weapons you can use to combat an injury or illness, the better. The more skills you know for promoting good health, the less susceptible you will be. Using your mind to stimulate the body's natural self-healing mechanisms is one way to take command of your physical problems. It gives you a method for working actively on your own behalf. It can't possibly hurt, and the benefits are surprising.

Mind over Cancer: One Woman's Story

The story of Emily Manning's astounding experience with—and triumph over—breast cancer is a remarkable example of how one woman's strength and perseverance helped her mind to heal her body. It started in 1986, when Emily's father died suddenly and unexpectedly of lung cancer. His passing was particularly shocking for Emily because the cancer had been undetected until it spread throughout his body. Only when doctors found an inoperable brain tumor did they realize that cancer was present.

Emily resolved not to suffer the same fate. As part of her personal cancer-prevention plan she faithfully had a mammogram and Pap smear every six months. And her caution paid off when one mammogram revealed a nickel-sized lump in her right breast. When a second mammogram, a sonogram, and a needle aspiration confirmed the presence of a tumor (rather than a cyst), Emily's doctors recommended an immediate biopsy to determine if the tumor was malignant and, if it was, whether a mastectomy would be necessary.

"It's not possible for me to have the biopsy right away," Emily said. She was due to leave for Maine the next day to visit a dear friend who, by a horrible coincidence, was dying of brain cancer. Nothing was going to stop Emily from saying her last goodbyes. "Can we do the biopsy next week?" she asked. Unfortunately, her doctor was going to be out of town that week. Neither she nor Emily felt comfortable about delaying surgery for two weeks, but Emily was firm.

Little did either of them know that by postponing the procedure Emily would have the opportunity to heal herself. As a recent graduate of the Free Soul course, Emily had learned the techniques of self-healing. She resolved to use the time before the scheduled surgery to try to reduce and remove the tumor. Five times a day she sent her mind traveling within her body to the site of the growth. Once there, she visualized withdrawing energy from the tumor. She mentally ordered her white blood cells and immune system to attack it vigorously, to break it down and carry it away. Next, she projected throughout her body thoughts aimed at forcing other cells in the area to develop normally. "I'm not going to let cancer beat me like it beat my dad," she told herself. "I'm going to use every physical and spiritual resource I have."

Emily doubled and redoubled her self-healing efforts. Each day when she woke, and at breakfast, lunch, dinner, and bedtime Emily worked mentally to attack the tumor. Each time she visualized energy being drawn from the tumor and mentally directed the immune system to attack it, she felt a burning, slightly painful sensation in the area of the lump. Each time, that is, except the last day before she was due at the hospital. As she did her self-healing that day she felt nothing—she sensed only smooth-flowing energy in her breast.

Next day in the operating room Emily's doctor took one final mammogram to get an exact fix on the tumor's location.

To the technician's surprise the growth could not be located. Five hours, several technicians, and several mammograms later, still no tumor could be found. The doctors had no explanation, but Emily did. She had used her mind and her God-given talents to help her body heal itself.

Emily's story is just one of literally hundreds telling how Free Soul graduates used advanced mind-body control to help heal themselves. Some victories were minor, such as overcoming allergies or asthma. Some were remarkable, like one woman's ability to regenerate a nerve in her leg. Some show courage and determination, such as one man's walk to the nearest town on a partially fractured leg. Some even went against the plans of the patient. That last story still makes me smile when I think about the mind's self-healing potentials.

Healed Though He Didn't Want It

Joe was the kind of student who gives an instructor fits. A total skeptic, he said he was taking our course only to learn ESP well enough to make a fortune gambling. He didn't want anything to do with "the rest of the kooks and weirdos" in the class. Joe always wore T-shirts and jeans to class; it was five weeks before he took off his sunglasses.

I met Joe for the first time soon after his class graduated. The first thing he said to me was, "You know, you cost me $50,000! It's all your fault. I tried that self-healing technique and it cost me a bunch of money. I was in an auto accident and damaged some vertebrae in my neck. I had X-rays and everything. The accident really wasn't the other guy's fault, but I knew I had a great opportunity to stick it to him and his insurance company. I was ready to sue for all I could get when we had the class on self-healing. I figured I would try it so I'd know how to fix myself after I got the money. When I went to the insurance company's doctor for verifying X-rays, they didn't show any damage at all. I didn't have any more pain. I lost a bundle."

It seems there is poetic justice after all. Joe, for the life of him, couldn't understand why I was laughing. "I suppose it was worth learning what I could do, but I'm sure going to miss that money," he said.

Never Underestimate the Power of Your Mind

Science still does not fully understand all the mechanisms of self-healing. But we do know that the unleashed mind can do far more than was previously thought. Under hypnosis, people turn off pain and stop bleeding. Yogis can stop the heart and raise skin temperature. Ordinary people like Emily and Joe can direct the body's immune system and regenerative mechanisms to heal themselves. Now it is your turn to gain these skills.

Learning to consistently affect the correct nerve cells and their interconnections won't happen instantly. It takes practice and discipline. Remember, however, that even small gains are steps forward. Don't limit the possibilities. In time your skills will sharpen and unlimited control of your physical body will become a reality for you.

Inner Vitalization: Unleashing the Mind in the Body

Thus far you have learned two-thirds of the skills necessary for effective self-healing. You know how to enter the involuntary nervous system by triggering Auto-Relaxation. You know how to gently guide your focused awareness to any bodily location. The final skill is knowing what to do when you get there.

While we do not yet fully understand how the mind stimulates the immune system and cell regeneration, we do know that combining visualization with a multisensory approach yields the best results. Seeing, feeling, knowing, and understanding the image of the body changing as you want it to change is the strongest mental signal you can send. When that signal is sent from within the tissue itself, the effect is almost unstoppable. Don't limit yourself in the way you visualize that signal being transmitted. William S. Kroger, M.D., and William D. Felzer, Ph.D., in their work with imagery and biofeedback, found that the more bizarre the visualization, the stronger the physical effect. Sometimes the more intangible the image visualized, the more readily it is accepted by the unconscious mind.

In Free Soul we have found that a three-step method for sending that signal works best. First, radiate energy outward from within the area itself. Second, pull energy from the universe to you to bombard and irradiate the area. Third, see, feel, know, and understand every cell, every fiber, every part of the area becoming perfect. Experience this three-step method for yourself now. Choose one of your hands—the one you feel is not as strong as the other. (We use the hands in practicing this because their high degree of sensitivity lets you quickly feel the effect you generate.)

1. Sit or lie comfortably, and close your eyes.

2. Unwind by using your Relaxation Breath Pattern and repeat the procedures you learned in the technique for taking that inner voyage into your body.

3. Gently let your total awareness move downward into your body, and to the hand you picked as less strong.

4. Once there, take a moment to fully experience the different tissues and energies in your hand. Feel the muscles, bones, blood vessels, ligaments, skin. Sense the overall level of vitality or energy of your hand, noting any strengths or weaknesses.

5. Now more than before, feel yourself fully within your hand. Begin to attract healing, vitalizing, and strengthening energy to yourself. Feel the hand being surrounded by flowing light and energy. See it being charged and bombarded by beams of force from outside.

6. From your awareness inside your hand, radiate energy outward. See and feel healthy, strengthening, and vitalizing energy being directed from within and deposited in all parts of the hand.

7. As this two-way energy vitalization is taking place, feel the overall energy level and vitality of your hand increasing. Picture every aspect of your hand becoming perfect and strong. See the muscles becoming lean and vigorous. Sense the bone growing solid and sturdy. Feel the joints being flexible and well lubricated. Project the thought of the blood vessels being clear and resilient.

8. When you feel you have carried out this vitalization process long enough, gradually return to your normal state of awareness and open your eyes. Without moving too much, compare the difference in feeling between your two hands.

How did you do? Does the hand you vitalized feel stronger and sounder than the other one? Does it feel different from its original state? Flex both hands and see if you feel a difference. Did you realize you could create such a noticeable effect in minutes? Think of what you could do with regular practice and discipline! Begin now to put this new skill to work for you. Pick an area of your body that you want to vitalize. Go to that area and repeat the process above. Notice the difference you feel.

Crossing the Threshold to Your Full Potential

There is no limit to the number of ways you can explore and practice mind-body control and inner healing vitalization. With the skills you have now learned you have the ability to create a new you. You can defeat the negative effects of stress before they strike. You can control your body's fight-or-flight reflex in critical or emergency situations. And you can stimulate your entire physical being to greater vitality and health.

Even so, you have barely crossed the threshold to the realm of mind power. As amazing as mind-body control is, it pales by comparison with what we shall explore next—the mind's ability to enter the universe of energy and the dimensions beyond the physical.

• 8 •

You Are a Soul That Has a Body—Exploring Deeper Dimensions

YOU ENTER a small theater. The lights are turned low. On the stage a man stands atop a huge electrical coil. He holds a wooden paddle in his hands. A switch is thrown, generators come to life, a whirring sound is heard, and suddenly a million volts of electricity pass around and through the man's body. Arcs of blue lightning spring from his hands to the board he holds. A jagged streak of electric flames burns up the paddle. After what seems like hours but is actually less than a minute, the man shouts, "Off!" The whirring stops, the crackling of electricity ceases, the arcs of blue lightning no longer leap from his fingers. In his hands the board still flames and smoulders along the jagged burn scar that marks the path the million volts had run after passing from his body.

Why is the man still alive? How can he still be standing? How can his body withstand the shock of a million volts without his being instantly electrocuted? As he steps off the electrical coil and hands the charred paddle to an awestruck onlooker, he begins to explain.

The electricity was out of tune with his body. Though the voltage was incredibly high, it was at a frequency that does not harm human tissue. It resonated at a level different from the vibrations of his physical cells. "Perhaps," he speculates, "the same is true of the Soul, God, and other things spiritual. Perhaps they are actually right here with us, but out of phase, out of sync, or in a different dimension from the physical reality we are used to."

Have you seen this million-volt demonstration? It has been performed frequently at one or another of the World's Fairs in the last thirty years. I first saw it in Seattle at the 1962 World's Fair, and later in New York in 1964. I was no less amazed when I saw it a third time, years later, at the Spokane, Washington, Expo Fair. I was amazed not just by the spectacle itself, but by the theory propounded to account for it. It was my first exposure to the concept that science and spirituality need not be enemies—that the two can coexist, that one can explain the other, that they can be two sides of the same coin.

My experiences at MIT only served to deepen my conviction that the concept is valid. I mentioned earlier that many aspects of modern science are stranger than metaphysics, stranger even than the world of the psychic. My goal was to point out that things that seem unbelievable are not necessarily untrue. Time and again as I studied chemistry, physics, and brain science, I was faced with scientific facts and ideas that seemed to defy common sense.

For example, quantum physics states that it is impossible to know exactly where an electron is, only where it may be. Relativity teaches that as objects move faster they become shorter, and time slows down for them. Chemistry tells us that all diamonds—even those cut and polished into gem stones—are unstable compounds and will eventually turn into common graphite. Fortunately for jewelry lovers, the process takes thousands of years because the threshold of reaction is so high. Each of these concepts is contrary to everyday experience, yet science proved them to be true. I began to realize that truth and reality frequently lie beyond the reach of the physical senses and everyday logic.

Equally mystifying was another aspect of my study of brain science. In it I learned just how much science doesn't know about the most important field of all, human potential—you, who you are, and how you function. After a century of studying and using hypnosis, for instance, we still don't understand exactly how it can control pain, evoke forgotten memories, and even cause blisters to develop by the mere suggestion of being burned. What struck me most, however, was the realization that science has no explanation for what the mind is or how creative thought is initiated. That point was made dramatically clear to me one spring afternoon during my senior year at MIT.

The Day Brain Science Was Not Enough

I was fortunate that semester to have a one-on-one tutorial with Dr. Whitman Richards, a senior professor in the department of brain science and physiological psychology. Two years earlier I had taken his course in the psychology of perception. In it we studied how the brain and the physical senses function. I remember clearly one particular lecture. Professor Richards was explaining how cells in a region of the brain called the motor strip had been identified as responsible for muscle contraction and movement. If a specific cell is stimulated electrically, a specific muscle will move or a leg will jerk. If a person voluntarily moves that muscle, that cell can be seen to fire. All around me fellow classmates were nodding their heads and saying, "Ah, now we understand." But I was not satisfied.

I understood the physiology being discussed, but it did not

explain to me how we consciously choose to move and act. Two years later, speaking with Professor Richards in his laboratory, I pursued my question. "What makes that brain cell fire when we decide to move an arm or a leg?" I asked him. "What triggers the electrical activity that stimulates the nerve and muscles?"

"Some other brain cell connected to it," he answered. But that only led me to ask the obvious next question: "What makes *that* cell fire?" Again he said, "Some other cell connected to it." And of course I repeated my question.

This intellectual merry-go-round continued until I finally said, "Come on, Professor Richards, stop avoiding the issue. What first starts the whole chain?"

"I have to believe it's some cells in our sensory inputs of vision, hearing, touch, and so on," he said.

"You're telling me that brain science believes human beings are nothing more than reactions to stimuli we get through our physical senses? That we never act voluntarily, only react automaticallly?"

"Well, more like reactions bounced off a highly sophisticated memory storage," he said.

"That means we're nothing more than robots reacting to the world around us," I said. "Don't you feel that you have some control, that you have volition, that you make decisions? Don't you feel that you initiate thoughts?"

Richards finally said, "Yes, I do feel I have choice and can initiate thoughts." I asked how the cells of the brain make that happen. "We don't know," he admitted.

To this day science cannot answer that question. Despite the breakthroughs made in neurology, brain science, and cell structure, we still do not know the source of consciousness. Science is at a loss to explain how you think, how you recognize yourself as a unique individual. We know how the brain reacts to stimuli; we know how your decisions are converted to actions and carried out by the nervous system. But how you *initiate* creative thought remains a mystery.

Defining the Term Soul

The creative part of you, that uniqueness that recognizes your self as an individual, is what I call the Soul. It is that part of you that is your identity. I believe it is the part above and beyond the wiring and the physical structure of the brain. To me the word *soul* is not necessarily a religious term. I use it as a label to summarize that complete, conscious, creative you. Whether you are deeply religious, an atheist, or an agnostic, you have a unique consciousness. It is the essence of your humanity.

You are going to learn in this chapter revolutionary methods for exploring that essence, and for experiencing the unlimitedness of the Soul part of you. Is it impossible to explore something science does not understand? No. In 1492 the idea that the world was round was an unproven theory. Even so, Columbus sailed off and changed history. He didn't wait for geographers to prove his journey would be possible. He didn't wait for inventors to discover a way to measure the earth's curvature. He pioneered.

You can pioneer in the same way, by boldly accepting the challenge to explore the world of the Soul and the unique consciousness you call You. Whether you believe consciousness is some deeply buried function of the brain, or that it exists in a dimension beyond the physical world, you *do* possess it. Anything you have, you can self-explore. You can—and will—learn a method for tapping your Soul energy. You can—and will—discover the pathway by which to extend your Soul energy into matter, light, and the far corners of the universe. You can—and will—learn how to use the Soul to access heightened consciousness and increased creativity. Most important, you can—and will—learn to cross the portal of the Soul to reach unlimitedness.

The Superstring Theory

Science and spirituality recently took a giant leap to close the gap between them with the development of a new theory of the universe and subatomic physics. It is called the Superstring Theory, and it promises to end the scientific search for a unified theory that explains mathematically the structure and relationship of all the forces and particles that exist in the cosmos, from the smallest subatomic particles to gravity and nuclear attraction.

What connects Superstring Theory to the exploration of consciousness and the Soul is the fact that its mathematical foundation requires the existence of ten dimensions. Physicists are coming to accept that all things—a chair, a lion, a planet, even you—exist in ten dimensions rather than the four we are familiar with (the three spatial dimensions of height, breadth, and length, plus the fourth dimension of time). The other six dimensions are still beyond our ability to identify, much less to measure with current technology.

The concept of other dimensions is not new. The term "hyperspace" existed long before George Lucas and his film *Star Wars.* Astronomers and astrophysicists have long proposed that the material being sucked into black holes may actually be compressed and shot through an extradimensional "back door" to distant portions of the universe—or even other universes—where it emerges from white holes. The key point is that Superstring Theory applies extradimensionality to *all of us,* not just to black holes or to science-fiction stories. Perhaps the unique consciousness that is you—the Soul you—exists in some of those added dimensions.

The Search for the Location of the Soul

Although we can't yet locate those other dimensions, we can experience them psychically, since each of the psychic senses is a window into the dimensions that lie beyond our physical senses. I am convinced that the Soul and your consciousness actually exist in many of those dimensions.

My strongest psychic ability—my clearest window on other dimensions—is Aura Vision. I have seen and studied thousands of auras for more than twenty years. From that study I have determined the location of the Soul. As a result I can show you how to identify your own Soul energy, and how to tap it to reach the dimensions beyond.

If I had to describe a three-dimensional location for the Soul, it would be an area above and slightly behind the head. If you extend a line from your chin through the top of your head, it will bisect the energy field of your Soul Nature. This is the strongest part of the aura and the easiest to see. Most people see their first aura around and above the head area because they perceive the stronger Soul energy field rather than just the body's biomagnetic field. That is why paintings of saints and major religious figures always portray the halo there.

Imagine an upside-down iceberg. It provides a good analogy for the relationship of the Soul's energy to the body. The bulk of an iceberg lies below water; only about a tenth of it rides above the surface. Turn this image upside down and you have a rough view of the Soul's relationship to the body. Most of the energy that you are as a Soul exists *outside* the body (above the head and slightly behind it), much like the larger, normally underwater part of the iceberg. The smaller part of the iceberg (normally above the water) is equivalent to the part of the Soul's energy that extends down into the head area, links up with the brain and physical senses, and coordinates the machinery of the body.

For most of your life you focus your awareness down through the body and out through your physical senses. To tap and experience the deeper dimensions of your Soul, you need to learn to reverse that focus up and out to the more extensive portion of Soul energy above the head. In Free Soul we call this making a Soul-shift. This upward focus shift is what happens when people meditate successfully. You can see it happen when you watch their aura. Around the chest and face the aura dims while above the head it expands, deepens, and moves farther away from the body.

The Soul-Shift and Alpha-Brain-Wave Connection

That change can also be measured scientifically. When you shift your focus up to the Soul area, your level of alpha-brain-wave activity markedly increases. This is significant because the alpha-brain-wave pattern has consistently been linked with higher forms of consciousness such as biofeedback, trance, self-hypnosis, and enhanced creativity. I was able to confirm this connection at a health fair in Glenwood Springs, Colorado, and thoroughly enjoyed myself in the process.

Every year a major television station sponsors health fairs throughout Colorado. At this particular one there was a booth on biofeedback that had a toy that I had been deprived of during my MIT years. It was a train that you could activate by generating alpha brain waves. I had seen them but had never been able to try one out.

Because I knew how to Soul-shift at will, I could slip in and out of "alpha" quickly. With electrodes taped to my head, I was able to run an electric train in a way I never could as a youngster. By mere thought I could make the train start and run at different speeds. By shifting down from the Soul I could stop it in an instant—at the water tower, at the station, or, to be perverse, inside the tunnel. The operators of the exhibit were astonished at my ability to quickly generate and easily control alpha brain waves. They thought the alpha state could be reached only by slow and steady meditation. That day their thinking was changed and I was able to verify the clear link between the alpha-brain-wave pattern and tapping the Soul.

Tuning Your Mind for the Jump to Hyperspace

You now know the location of your Soul energy. Tapping that energy requires learning a pathway for reaching it and a method for attuning your mind to it. The simplest pathway is a mental elevator. As you ride it, gradually shift your focus up through the body and then take a final mental step out into your unlimited Soul energy.

Do not try, force, or overconcentrate while making these shifts of awareness. This applies to all forms of mental and psychic exploration, but particularly to tapping the Soul. Force does nothing to speed your journey. It is usually more detrimental than helpful because it increases your level of physical tension and keeps you from the relaxed and open form of consciousness required for extradimensional exploration. In scientific terms, when you try or force, your alpha-brain-wave activity drops drastically. Intense concentration pushes you into brain-wave patterns more typical of routine activity than of higher consciousness.

The stereotypes you see in movies or on television, where people squeeze their eyes shut, hold their heads, and strain in concentration to sense psychically or tap higher consciousness are completely inaccurate. The correct method is to focus your awareness lightly and guide it gently but firmly.

The key word is *focus:* to selectively heighten your awareness along the inner direction you are exploring, allowing it to flow along the path of your search. As I pointed out in other sections of this book, the difference between focusing and forcing is similar to the difference between peripheral vision and staring. Staring has an intensity and pressure to it. Seeing something with peripheral vision is more gentle; it requires you to focus your awareness at the sides, heightening your attention there. You are *noticing rather than forcing.* To experience your Soul, learn to focus your awareness gently, like an inner form of peripheral vision.

Tapping the Extradimensionality of the Soul

The process outlined below will guide you in making that upward shift and in exploring the fullness of your Soul energy. The effect is like a slingshot, propelling you up and out to your own deeper dimensions. You will feel boundaries dissolve as you step into this more expansive part of your being. You will feel the peace and heightened awareness available to you there. Do not try to analyze what you are sensing during the technique. That will only create tension and cut off or limit your experience. Review your impressions later.

1. Relax, sit or lie comfortably, and close your eyes. Slip into your Relaxation Breath Pattern to release any tensions.
2. Gradually increase awareness of yourself rather than of your environment. Do not try or concentrate, but gently focus your awareness of what you are feeling from and within yourself.
3. Next, pay specific attention to your lower legs. Sense your feet, your ankles, your calves. Slowly begin to shift your focus up through your legs, hips, waist, chest, shoulders. As you sense each body area and are moving upward, gradually leave behind the parts you have already sensed. Tune them out. Ride this mental elevator upward until you reach the head area.
4. As you focus on the head, take time to feel all the

thoughts and memories that are you. Briefly let yourself see what comes to mind when you focus on yourself as a person.

5. Shift your focus one more level upward to the Soul area. Some people experience this final focus-shift as a feeling of stepping out of the top of their heads. Notice how the boundaries seem to disappear and you feel as if you are in an expanding dimension. Feel your awareness of yourself deepen, as if you have stumbled onto a seldom-explored but richer part of yourself. You may even feel you can extend outward limitlessly in any direction. This is the Real You. You have become aware of your Soul Nature.

Note: If you feel any pressure in your forehead or eye area as you make this final focus-shift, you are probably trying to turn your eyes backward and force them to look out of the back of your head. They will not go there. Leave them where they belong. Make that final focus-shift more a feeling of letting your mind float, or a heightened awareness of the space above you.

6. Explore this deeper part of yourself. See how far you can extend outward. Sense how ageless you feel. Experience the peacefulness that radiates through you as you tap the extra dimensions of your Soul.

7. When you are finished, gently shift your focus back down to the head area and note some specific part of your body (nose, mouth, hands). Slowly move a finger or foot, and when you feel ready, open your eyes. Gently move your body to restore your normal physical orientation.

This technique is only the first step on a long and fascinating journey into the extra dimensions of the Soul. The more you meditate and practice the process, the easier it will be to tune out distractions. The more you experience your Soul, the easier it will be to make that final up-and-out focus-shift. Exploring your extra dimensions can also be a natural relaxer. Tapping the Soul even briefly relieves the pressure of the physical world. In most instances one's aura will unwind and expand two to six inches by the time the exercise is completed. Once you learn control, the Soul-shift can be used at will throughout your day.

Tapping the Soul's Unlimited Creativity

Whether it is due to increased alpha-brain-wave activity or to the linkup between your spiritual and physical energies, the shift of awareness to the Soul level, to your superconscious state, allows you to initiate heightened creativity whenever you need it. You can command at will access to a whole new dimension of information and awareness. Nationwide, Free Soul graduates are reaching new levels of success because they have learned how to go that one step beyond.

Mimi Miller of Del Mar, California, is a teacher, the mother of two children, and the founder of a creative children's products company. David Pierce of Silver Spring, Maryland, is a statistician with the Federal Reserve Board. Their lives and professions are worlds apart, but as Free Soul instructors they share the common bond of knowing how to Soul-shift. David's first experience with higher consciousness occurred when he inadvertently Soul-shifted while working on his doctorate in statistics. The insights that became his thesis broke through in a brief period of heightened awareness, providing solutions to equations that had stumped him for months. Today David uses his enhanced potential to design statistical models for economic forecasting. Although his work is more intellectual than artistic, it still requires creativity. Intuitively knowing which statistical method will make a successful forecasting tool is the key to the accurate economic predictions his job requires.

Mimi uses her Soul-shifting skills to enhance a different kind of creativity. Working with colors and shapes to develop innovative products for children, Mimi turned what began as a homecraft hobby into a successful business. Recently the firm that produced Mimi's designs was taken over by a major corporation. With expansion of her business, pressures began to mount, and Mimi could feel her creative flow shutting down. Tension built to the point where she felt totally blocked when trying to come up with ideas for new products. The deadline for the next year's line of children's wall hangings was near, and Mimi didn't have a single idea. She felt she had seen and designed every imaginable type of wall hanging.

When she could delay no longer, Mimi forced herself into her studio, resolved to break her mental block. Dropping into her Relaxation Breath Pattern and shifting up to her Soul, she could sense her burnt-out feeling starting to dissipate. Excitement began to fill her. Within minutes she saw in her mind a series of wall hangings that glow in the dark. One was a teddy bear that poured a bucket of rainbows by day and rained down glowing stars by night. Another was a daytime sun that became a crescent moon at night. Mimi's "Day and Night" line proved to be one of the most popular items at an annual exhibition of new products for children.

Do You Have a Soul?

I am sure that *soul* is a term most of you are comfortable with. All major religions include within their framework the concept of the Soul. Whether it is called Soul, Spirit, Atman, or Intelligent Energy, the meaning is still the same. From a scientific point of view, you may think of the Soul as being a unique energy pattern or field that lies beyond the transience of physical matter, and outside the limited forms of currently measurable energy. In terms of the Superstring Theory, it would be those additional six dimensions we all have.

Most people I meet readily admit they believe they have a Soul. This is not enough. To tap your full potential you must go beyond this. You do not *have* a Soul. You *are* a Soul. You *are* a Soul that *has* a body. This is more than mere linguistics. It is the realization that the real You, your true self, is that Soul Nature—the conscious, initiating energy beyond the wiring and machinery of the physical body.

In fact, the belief that you *have* a Soul is one of the prime causes of people's limitations. If you *have* a Soul, then *you* must be something else. That something else you identify with is the physical body. As a result, you impose on yourself all the physical limitations we have been trying to go beyond. Just as the car that you drive is but a tool you use for travel, so your physical body is only an extension of the inner driver that is the Soul. You are the controller, not the controlled machinery. You are the water in the glass, not the glass. You are the electricity that runs the machine, not the motor. You *are* a Soul. You *have* a body.

Don't let yourself be trapped into limitations. See yourself as a Soul. Feel yourself as a Soul. Understand and know that your true nature is to be unlimited. Never underestimate how strongly our societal programming has trained us to think of ourselves in a limited way. Even our language leads us away from the concept that we *are* Souls by causing us to say, "my Soul," when it would be more correct to say, "I Soul."

Now you have a way of breaking the bonds of physical limitations. Experiencing your Soul Nature and being able to make that Soul-shift at will are major steps on the path to full spiritual freedom. You no longer have to confine yourself to the physical limitations of the body. You now have personal experience with the reality of "something beyond."

The Unlimited Nature that Is a Soul

Learning to tap your Soul is the gateway to the unlimited potentials that are your birthright. Through it you enter a realm of infinitely flexible energy. Indeed, you *are* energy. Einstein's $E = mc^2$ equation states that energy equals mass times the speed of light squared. In nonmathematical terms that means all things are energy, only they appear in different forms. The chair is energy. Light is energy. You are energy.

The law of conservation of energy states, "Energy can neither be created nor destroyed, only changed in form." That means that you, as energy, are now, always have been, and always will be. The only question is what you will do with your energy. Will you limit and suppress it? Or will you reach for your unlimitedness?

The first way to prove to yourself the unlimitedness of your Soul energy is to expand your awareness beyond the constrictions of physical boundaries. One of the advantages of realizing that you *are* a Soul that *has* a body is that you no longer limit yourself to purely physical capabilities; you have the ability to blend and be one with all things.

Slipping the Shackles of the Body

Because we tend to think of ourselves as the distinct physical entity of our bodies, we tend to separate ourselves from other objects, people, and environments. While it is true that these are separate islands of matter, through your Soul Nature you can be at one with anything in your environment. You can blend into any object and sense it as an extension of yourself. You can gradually become a part of more and more around you.

As with Soul-shifting, the key to success is not trying or forcing. Relax and feel, gently extend, dropping one artificial boundary after another. Not only does this increase your sense of unlimitedness, but it is a bridge to deeper forms of psychic sensing. Here is the process for experiencing this Soul skill:

1. Sit comfortably and close your eyes. Slip into your Relaxation Breath Pattern and then shift your focus up to your Soul energy.

2. Gently float and enjoy the feeling of You, your Soul Nature. After a short while, allow that awareness to expand so that it gradually includes your whole being. Feel the real You becoming one with your physical body. Feel your body melt and blend into your awareness of yourself. At this point you may be experiencing for the first time the complete fullness of your total self—body, mind, and Soul. You should feel like one big ball of awareness, extending beyond the limits of your body but paradoxically penetrating deeper into the fabric of your physical being than you normally experience.

3. Allow your awareness to expand again so that it gradually includes all of the chair you are sitting in. Feel your arms melting into the arms of the chair; feel your back gently sinking into the energy of the chair. Feel yourself and the chair becoming one, so that your awareness now includes yourself, your physical being, and the chair.

4. Once you feel at one with the chair, explore it. What does it feel like inside? Can you sense all its parts—legs, back, under the seat? Can you feel where the chair touches the floor or the carpet?

5. Allow your awareness to expand again. This time blend along the carpet or floor to all corners of the room. Sense the other objects that come in contact with the floor and blend with them. Explore.

6. When you have finished exploring, gradually return your awareness to your body. Focus on a specific physical area like the nose, mouth, or hands, and when you feel ready, open your eyes. Gently move to restore your normal physical orientation.

Many people experience this blending haphazardly when they are tired, deeply relaxed, or when they meditate. It is, however, a capability that can be learned, controlled, and used in any situation and at any time.

Soul-Blending for Psychic Safety Checks

One of the most practical uses for Soul-blending is to sense psychically a structure or machine from the inside to spot defects or weaknesses. It can help you pick the best product, or tell if repairs have been properly performed. It can even identify potential life-threatening dangers. Some years ago, for instance, I used energy blending and advanced psychic sensing to ensure the safety of my family's trip from New York to Arizona. We were to drive a seven-year-old station wagon and I was concerned about how it would fare during the trip, especially since it would be loaded with household possessions and a crammed six-foot-long storage carrier on the roof rack.

I did all the standard things common sense dictates, from a complete mechanical inspection to an oil change. But there was one last safety check I wanted to do before we started out: I wanted to examine the car psychically. Sitting in the driver's seat, I shifted into a oneness with my Soul energy and began to blend into the fabric and material of the car. Dropping one boundary after another, I let my mind flow into the matter that made up the station wagon. I flowed into the frame and the body, felt that it was strong and solid. I sensed into the engine and knew that the motor would operate properly for the whole trip. Finally, I let my energy flow into the tires. There I sensed trouble.

From within the tires I saw two cracks of light that indicated weaknesses to me. One was in the tube of the right front tire, the other in a sidewall of the relatively new tubeless left rear tire. After returning to my normal physical orientation, I visually checked all four tires and measured the pressure in each of them. Everything appeared in order, but my psychic impressions from within were too strong to ignore. As a result, I bought a spare tube for the front tire and resolved to keep a watch on the others, particularly the left rear tire.

Only hours before we left New York the tube of the right front tire blew out. The rip was too large to be patched, but having the spare tube in hand meant we didn't have to delay our trip. As we traveled, I checked that left rear tire even more than the others. I was thankful I did. On the second night of our trip I was drawn to look under the car and noticed an inch-long split on the inside sidewall. I was amazed the tire hadn't already completely disintegrated. Had I headed out the next morning on that tire, the split would have shredded it. With the weight we were carrying, the car would undoubtedly have flipped over. Fortunately, we pulled into a repair shop just before it closed for the weekend, bought a replacement tire, and were on our way on schedule the next day.

This is a direct example of how the Soul's ability to extend and blend led directly to a heightened form of psychic sensitivity that proved invaluable. Think of what this ability could do for you. Imagine the extra information, safety, and security it could give you. Pick something in the next day or two and practice your ability to check it by sensing psychically from within.

Here is a partial list of some common items to which you can apply psychic scanning and checking from within:

- Clothes (for durability of fabric, seams, and color)
- Appliances before purchase (for defects not covered by warranty)
- Houses or apartments (for structural and wiring problems or insect pests)
- Used cars or other machinery (for weak areas and impending trouble)

- Ailing plants and animals (for the real cause of their dysfunction)
- Children (for the cause of their emotional or physical discomfort)

Blending with Energy and Light

The spiritual energy that comprises the Soul is remarkably flexible. Blending with matter is only the first step of what the Soul can do. You can also blend with pure energy and extend your awareness to greater depths. Learning to blend with forms of everyday energy such as heat and light is a key part of advanced control of the Soul's ability to blend and expand.

Learning to blend and be one with physical objects (your body, the chair, the car) gives you beginning experience with focused, directional expansion. Energy-blending helps you experience expansion in all directions simultaneously. It is the gateway for reaching complete oneness with the universe.

Most of the time your Soul energy is relatively focused. This natural concentration is necessary to allow you to function through a physical body. The secret to controlling Soul expansion and to experiencing the Soul's ability to blend without limits is to relax that Soul focus. As you do, you will feel your Soul naturally expanding from boundary to boundary. The more you relax, the further the expansion. You will feel an inner peace and security deeper than any you may have experienced.

"You literally feel one with the All," said William, who when I first met him had "dropped out" of conventional life soon after getting his degree in business and computer science. The rat race of the corporate world made him tense and unhappy.

At first William searched for contentment by studying

world religions. He wanted to feel connected, a part of the universe, at one with his vision of God. William even flirted with various Eastern cults, but chanting on a street corner didn't bring him inner peace. Finally he divorced himself from society. Selling his possessions, he bicycled across the U.S. for a year, searching for a way to feel one with the stars he saw in the clear night skies.

William was near the end of his bike trip when he attended one of my lectures. He was intrigued that someone else with a technical background was searching for unlimitedness as he was. That curiosity kept him coming back until he learned about the Universe Blend Meditation. After that William never had to search or travel again. He had found a way to reach what he called "Home." In a few short minutes he learned how to expand the boundaries of his Soul energy and journey to oneness with the stars. He came back feeling more at peace than ever before. What amazed him most was that it didn't take an hour of meditation or chanting, and he hadn't needed to find that perfect spot in the mountains.

The key for William had been learning Free Soul's technique of blending with light. He could understand light as energy that was truly unlimited. Riding its beams helped him take the limits off his consciousness for the first time. "I can find light anywhere. I don't have to keep searching for a path to follow to the stars. I can let them come to me wherever I am," he said. William has since returned to society and founded a successful computer software company. He balances the pressures by being able to take a Universe Blend break whenever he chooses.

Blending with the Universe

Beyond the boundaries of matter, blending with light is the next skill to learn. You can see light, you can feel its warmth. Because it is real and familiar to you, light is the easiest form of energy to blend with. Moreover, since light reaches everywhere, you can ride its waves to every corner of the universe. You can literally be one with all things. This next technique takes the Soul-blending ability you learned earlier and extends it to universal dimensions. Read the process below and then sit back and enjoy your ride to the stars.

1. Relax, sit comfortably, and close your eyes. Slip into your Relaxation Breath Pattern to release tensions and shift up to tune in to your Soul energy.

2. When you feel in harmony with yourself, begin to sense the light from the room as it falls on you. Feel its warmth and illumination.

3. Gradually become one with the light itself. As you feel it passing around you and through you, blend with it. Become a part of its warmth, radiance, expansiveness.

4. Being one with the light, travel with it. Extend into every corner of the room and fall upon every object. Go with the light and blend with all the areas it reaches. Feel at one with every part of the room and every object in it.

5. Next, sense your awareness extending beyond the room and including the whole building. Sense the different rooms and floors.

6. Now rise up and expand even farther. Stretch out to sense the whole neighborhood, and finally the entire city. Feel the various parts of the city as you know it: its center, its limits, the streets, the parks, the highways. Feel as if you have a thousand senses and can extend into all parts of the city at once. Be at one with the city and its people.

7. Again feel your awareness expanding. Let your being-ness spread until you cover your state or province, your nation, and finally the whole world. Feel yourself becoming one with the entire globe, at peace and in tune with its many

lands and oceans. Enjoy this sensation of being at one with our planet. Sense the deeper understanding and kinship you feel for all people on Earth.

8. Keep letting the boundaries dissolve. Let your being-ness expand even farther, blending with the solar system. Feel the other planets and the sun. Continue expanding past the solar system and to the Milky Way galaxy.

9. Completely release your beingness and feel yourself blending with the vastness of the universe, stretching to every portion of the cosmos, being one with every star and galaxy. Let yourself float and enjoy the total peace that is oneness with the universe.

10. After fully experiencing this oneness, gradually bring your awareness back to the galaxy, the solar system, the planet, your state, your city, the building, and yourself in your chair.

11. Specifically focus on a part of your body such as the nose, mouth, or hands. Gently move a finger or a foot, and when you are ready, open your eyes. Move easily to restore your normal physical orientation.

Doesn't that feel marvelous? Isn't it exciting to know you can go so far so quickly! Some people spend years meditating before they can reach that same level of macroconsciousness. Now you know how to be in harmony with the universe at any time in only a matter of minutes. The more you practice universe-blending, the easier it becomes. Once you are ex-perienced in the skill of Soul expansion you can quickly touch the peace of infinity whenever you wish. You can take a quantum leap in awareness whenever you need a larger perspective. No longer will you need to feel trapped by the pressures of living. Relief is as close as your next five-minute break. Try it during lunch or coffee the next few days and see how refreshed you feel.

You have now learned how to switch on your psychic

senses, to self-heal with mind-body control, and to expand your consciousness beyond all boundaries. With these skills you have truly crossed the threshold of a path toward unlimitedness. The next chapter completes this psychic road map: It will show you how to continue your journey and live as an unlimited Free Soul.

• 9 •

The Frontier Ahead—
The Road to Full Freedom

IT IS 11:45 P.M. on December 31, 1899, the turn of the century. In his laboratory, George sits in the time machine he has just finished building. A few hours earlier he demonstrated a miniature model of it to his friends. When it disappeared they thought it was a toy, or some kind of magic trick. Now George himself wants to go forward in time to see what frontiers lie ahead for mankind.

Nervous, but with resolve, he pushes the lever forward, and the steel dish behind him starts to spin. The years race ahead on his dials. Suddenly the time machine begins to shake and rock; the gauges cease to function. George is hurtling through time without knowing where he is. With great effort he reaches forward, grasps the control lever, and pulls it back, bringing the machine to such a sudden halt that it spins violently and throws George to the ground.

When he regains consciousness George finds himself in a

large room filled with people working in small groups. He moves among them to observe this future he has stumbled into. In one corner people are working on healing themselves, drawing Soul energy down into their bodies and irradiating their weakened areas from within. In another corner, people are practicing seeing and repairing auras. In still another part of the room George encounters people who are psychically sensing across vast distances of time and space. Everywhere he hears casual conversations about being bi-level—simultaneously seeing, sensing, and enjoying life in two interlocking universes. George wonders just how far into the future his runaway time machine has catapulted him.

This variation on H. G. Wells's classic story, *The Time Machine*, illustrates a point about psychic sensing that I want to emphasize. How far ahead has George traveled in time in my version of the story? Is he in the year 3000? Or the year 4000? No, George is here in our present—not quite a century since he left—and his machine has landed in the middle of a Free Soul retreat. The men and women around him are ordinary people like yourself, except for the fact that they have learned the skills for tapping the Soul and beyond.

Like George, you too stand on the threshold of a future that is already here. In this chapter you will learn about the new skills, the new horizons, the deeper dimensions that can enhance your future once you know how to cross the gateway to access your Soul energy. Through the experiences of Free Soul graduates you will see how you can weave into the fabric of your life the already phenomenal skills you have gained from earlier chapters. You will learn how to take your psychic sensitivity to a more useful level. You will discover how to tap your Soul with your eyes open, and to live life with bi-level consciousness.

Once you learn you *are* a Soul and know how to tap that higher consciousness, your perspective changes: You can sense on two levels simultaneously. Things you previously thought impossible or magical become simple and understandable. Your ability to sense psychically becomes easier and deeper. Even the techniques you have already learned will become doubly effective.

Advanced Healing Methods

Inner healing, for example, is directly enhanced after you know how to tap the Soul. By bringing the Soul down into the body you can radiate from within a form of energy unlimited in power. One of the reasons Emily was so successful in clearing her breast of its tumor was that she knew how to bring her complete Soul energy into her body. Rather than projecting only her thoughts to the area of the growth, she took her entire Soul on that inner voyage and projected its unlimited energy to assist in the healing.

You, too, can now Soul-shift and use this deeper form of healing. After reaching your Soul and sensing its bubble of expanded consciousness, mentally attach weight to the bubble and let the full expansiveness of your Soul energy sink down into the body, filling it from within like a light in a bottle. When you add this step to the inner healing technique, notice how your effectiveness increases. Knowing you are a Soul adds a new perspective to every skill you learn.

A New Form of Psychic Sensitivity

One of the tragedies of our world is that psychic gifts, or extrasensory perceptions, are believed to be unnatural or even evil phenomena. This misconception is one of the side effects of the belief that one is a body, rather than a Soul that *has* a body. If you believe that you are your physical body, it is logical that you will consider only your physical senses to be "normal." Anything else will seem strange, mystical, even frightening. When you believe you *are* a Soul your perception of what is "natural" becomes as unlimited as the Soul itself.

It is important here to review and reemphasize several main concepts that make up the basic framework of this new perspective:

- The physical body exists in the physical realm and has its own set of senses for discerning aspects of the physical world.

- You receive, understand, and apply these perceptions as a natural outcome of Soul-body relationship.

- Equally natural is the Soul's ability to sense independently of the body. These Soul senses are what have been called psychic gifts, or extrasensory perceptions (ESP). More accurately they are Higher Sensory Perceptions, or HSP, and they are just as natural, though far less limited, than your physical perceptions. There is nothing "extra" about them. Because each of us is a Soul, the Soul senses are available to us for practical use.

- Psychic senses are the natural way the Soul perceives the spiritual aspects of your environment—the energy patterns, vibrations, underlying feeling. By fully tapping these psychic senses you increase your awareness and begin to live the unlimited potentials you have as a Soul.

Up to now you have been taught to sense psychically only through the body, using the Psychic Reception Areas. In actuality, the Soul does not need to use the Psychic Reception Areas in order to tune in psychically. It is easier at first to learn psychic sensitivity using the Psychic Reception Areas because they are the strongest focal points within the physical body. But once you are able to sense the frequencies of the psychic gifts, you no longer need the Psychic Reception Areas to tune in to your ESP. You can psychically sense directly, as a Soul.

Experiencing Direct Psychic Sensitivity

In earlier chapters you learned the four ESP channels available to you. Now that you have some experience with them, and also know how to tap your Soul Nature, you can bypass the body's Psychic Reception Areas. You can sense on those four frequencies by shifting up to your Soul.

The technique described below gives you the opportunity to experience this advanced form of psychic sensitivity. Before you begin, realize that you already experienced psychic sensing as a Soul in the last chapter. When you made that final focus-shift, your physical body did not go with you. The impressions you received while Soul-shifting and blending came through the senses of your Soul. Now learn to refine your control of this skill:

1. Relax, sit or lie comfortably, and close your eyes. Repeat the procedures you have learned for shifting up to your Soul. Gradually tune out your environment and focus your awareness more on yourself. Steadily shift that focus up through the various parts of your body until you reach the head area. Then, as before, make the final focus shift up and out.

2. Feel once again the relaxed calm of your Soul energy. Take a moment to enjoy its peaceful unlimitedness. Sense how your awareness feels different, its range vastly increased, its scope more penetrating.

3. First, focus on your Soul ability to see. Tune in to your Psychic Vision. Gently, without forcing or trying, become aware of the 360-degree visual capability available to you on this higher level. See what images or impressions you can perceive. Note the softness, the more evanescent quality of this Soul Vision in contrast to physical vision.

4. Then, notice the sense of Psychic Feeling. Feel how this Soul sense is like a giant antenna picking up vibrations around you. Experience the depth of this sensation compared to physical feeling. Feel the ripples of the universe pass around and through you.

5. Next, tune to your Psychic Audience (hearing/listening). Do not so much try to hear as simply to listen and receive impressions. Grasp your ability to be a sensitive receiver of the thought waves of the universe. Compare your impressions with those of physical hearing.

6. Finally, access your Soul sense of knowing, Psychic Intuition. Relax, be conscious of the Soul's ability to be aware, to be an open funnel to the cosmos.

7. Return your focus to the center of your Soul Nature and experience the heightened sensitivity available through your Soul senses. Let all four psychic channels come to you simultaneously and experience total sensing as a Soul.

8. When you have finished, gradually shift your focus back more to your body than to your environment. When you feel comfortable, open your eyes. Stay relaxed and motionless. Without closing your eyes or specifically focusing on your Soul, recapture those same feelings of enhanced awareness and sensitivity you have just experienced. Identify how those abilities can be with you at all times.

The more you practice sensing as a Soul, the easier it becomes to tune in psychically either with or without the body. You will no longer be limited to sensing only through the Psychic Reception Areas. Knowing how to sense directly as a Soul also makes it easier to switch ESP channels. You can shift rapidly through all four psychic frequencies to compare notes or to verify an unclear impression. When your situation requires you to be completely physically present, you can still use the Psychic Reception Areas to amplify the psychic vibrations around you. When full physical attention is not required, you can sense directly as a Soul. In these instances you will find that your psychic senses are stronger, less masked by the static and disruptions of the body.

At first your impressions may be vague or fuzzy, but that is because you are not used to navigating on the Soul dimension. As you practice sensing as a Soul, the images will sharpen and the perceptions will become clearer. Two-way communication also becomes possible. Not only can you receive information through the higher Soul channels, you can also transmit messages over them.

Communing on the Soul Level

Since she was a young child, Ann Stacy Russell has known how to sense and communicate on the Soul level. She used to help her mother find misplaced items by shifting up and looking psychically. Time and again Ann found her mother's glasses and keys by tuning in to them from a Soul perspective and sensing what other objects or environment surrounded them. This gave her a picture of where to go to find the lost item.

These days, her talents honed by Free Soul studies, Ann uses her Soul level to communicate as well as receive, particularly in her work as a caregiver for two elderly women. Both Bertha and Doreen suffer the effects of advanced aging: Their hearing is no longer keen and their verbal skills have deteriorated. Ann finds that by projecting her thoughts psychically from the Soul level while she speaks, Bertha and Doreen understand her better. When the women have trouble speaking, Ann Soul-shifts to listen.

Sometimes, to comfort them and bring peace, Ann simply sits and communes with Bertha and Doreen from that higher level, holding hands and being with them Soul to Soul. This extra contact seems to bring an added sense of security to the lives of Bertha and Doreen.

Any situation where physical communication breaks down can be helped by sensing and transmitting from the Soul level. Like Ann, you can use the psychic senses of the Soul to better reach the elderly and infirm. Mothers often do this instinctively with their young children. The process is enhanced, however, when a parent consciously Soul-shifts and directs the contact.

Communication before Birth

It is even possible to communicate in this way with an unborn child. This was dramatically brought home to me when my wife, Debbie, was pregnant with our first son, Brian. Both Debbie and I felt a particularly close rapport with the Soul energy of Brian before his birth. As part of her prenatal preparations Debbie regularly meditated and did biofeedback work with the growing fetus. I frequently tuned in mentally to visit with and welcome my coming son.

One week, when I was traveling out of state on business, I had free time between appointments. Since it was about time for Debbie and me to decide on a name for the baby, I decided to visit with my son and ask him what he wanted to be called. In my hotel room I meditated, Soul-shifted, and traveled astrally back to Arizona. Connecting with the consciousness I recognized as my son's energy, I asked, "What name would you like?" Clearly I saw and distinctly I heard the name, *"Brian."*

When I returned home later that week I shared my experience with Debbie. She jumped with excitement, because during one of her inner travels to the uterus she too had asked, "What name would you like?" and intuitively received *"Brian."* The experience was particularly striking because Debbie and I had not previously talked about names for the baby, and neither of us had anyone in our families called Brian. The name was definitely Brian's own choosing.

The lessons of that early communication have continued

to unfold for Brian. Because much of my work entails traveling, often for weeks or a month at a time, I taught Brian how
to communicate on the Soul level. Before he was three years
old he could reach me mentally whenever he was lonely.
Once when Debbie felt blue and missed me, Brian said,
"Mom, you should talk to Dad more in your mind like I do.
Then you won't miss him."

Bi-level Awareness: A Quantum Leap in Consciousness

You don't have to sacrifice physical sensitivity in order to
tap the deep Soul skills. You can use both of them simultaneously. This is what I call Bi-level Awareness. Bi-level Awareness means being able to sense in and above the plane of the
physical world at the same time. It is something like being a
skindiver whose mask is right at the surface, and thus he can
see above and below the water simultaneously. When you
have mastered Bi-level Awareness you no longer need to
close your eyes or meditate to reach higher consciousness
and deeper Soul skills. You can go about your daily affairs as
always while at the same time being aware of the extra
dimensions available to you as pure Soul energy.

Learning Bi-level Awareness is neither hard nor complicated. All that is required is the determination to practice
the following technique until you have it firmly under your
control.

1. Relax, sit comfortably, and close your eyes. Repeat the
steps for shifting up to your Soul. As you make that final
focus-shift, feel your beingness expand as you sense your full
potential. Rest here for a moment feeling the unlimitedness
that is your total self.
2. While maintaining your focus in that Soul area, open

your eyes. See the environment around you, but keep your primary awareness focused on the sense of yourself as Soul energy. If you feel yourself losing control (you may feel your focus slipping back to the head area), briefly close your eyes and refocus up to your Soul. Then open your eyes and feel yourself able to maintain the bi-level state longer.

3. Next, keeping your primary awareness on your Soul Nature, stand up. If you feel your focus slipping a bit, retune it by increasing your awareness of the area above and slightly behind the head; or, if you need to, close your eyes, refocus, and open them again. Do not be afraid of losing your focus or having your awareness of your Soul slip a bit. First, expect the sensation to be less strong than it is with your eyes closed (because your other physical awarenesses are competing for attention). Second, realize that one of the purposes of this technique is to give you practice tuning to your Soul Nature from an eyes-open, physically active state. Try to maintain your Soul awareness, but if you lose it, simply practice your control and refocus.

4. Try walking slowly around the room while maintaining an awareness of your Soul energy. If you start to lose your focus, stop for a moment, retune, and continue. Gradually pick up your pace and experiment with how long it takes to lose or weaken your Soul awareness. Then slow down and refocus as you walk more gently.

5. Finally, take time to practice eyes-open Soul awareness during physical activity. If you can, get outside and walk in a safe area or around the halls of the building. Do not be afraid to look at or touch objects around you. Gradually increase the degree of your physical involvement with your surroundings while maintaining the same awareness and feeling of your Soul Nature. You can also practice blending and psychically sensing from this bi-level state.

6. When you are ready to stop, shift your focus more to your physical body and touch some part of your face. Flex your fingers rapidly to help ground yourself, and stroke your head lightly to restore your normal physical orientation.

This is just a beginning experience with tapping your Soul during eyes-open activity. But there is no limit. The more you practice control, the more you will find you can maintain a dual awareness of your physical and spiritual natures no matter what the extent of your physical involvement. The more you shift up to your Soul in daily activities, the better will be your ability to tap ESP on the move. You will find a greater sense of spiritual calm when you can go through your day knowing how to tune in to your Soul energy.

Touching Nirvana Through Bi-level Awareness

Tapping your Soul with your eyes open is an introduction to Bi-level Awareness. The next step is to experience bi-level blending. Follow the original procedure to achieve a mini Universe Blend and then open your eyes, stand, and move about the room. Focus on blending with the objects around you. With each step you take, feel your foot harmonizing with the floor or carpet. As you pass an object or plant, extend your beingness and be one with it. Continue to walk and extend your blending until you are literally walking in oneness with all things around you.

Many men and women—perhaps many of you who are reading this—spend years trying to reach this nirvana-like experience of walking in oneness, for it is a beautiful and near-religious sensation. Yet it is but one of many abilities that will be open to you through Bi-level Awareness; do not think of it as the ultimate skill. In Free Soul we use the expression "different skills for different situations." Being bi-levelly blended is not, for instance, the skill of choice when crossing a busy street; you might become permanently blended with a bus! Bi-level blending is primarily an excellent way to add pockets of peacefulness to your busy days.

The many facets of Bi-level Awareness bring the unlimited potentials of the Soul into all the areas of your life. Not only can you tap your unlimited energy, you can reach deeper levels of creativity and psychic sensitivity. Sensing psychically as a Soul in a bi-level way also enhances your ESP skills. The four anecdotes I'm going to tell you now show how tapping Bi-level Awareness and living life as a Soul can enhance the success and quality of your life.

Problem-Solving Through Bi-level Awareness

Scott Maley works for an international technical consulting company in Oklahoma City. As a computer systems analyst, Scott's main responsibility is troubleshooting. He comes to the rescue of businesses that are hopelessly tangled in Gordian knots of computer breakdowns and malfunctions. Scott's ability to access his full potential through Bi-level Awareness makes him a top-notch problem-solver. He is usually sent in only after other experts have failed.

Scott uses Bi-level Awareness to help him solve complex technical problems quickly and without complications. Before he became a Free Soul student and then instructor, Scott would chew over problems until he was exhausted. Bi-level Awareness enables him to shortcut the process.

"When I Soul-shift," he says, "the key data and possible solutions flow freely to my mind." For example, Scott recently was assigned to analyze the machines, software, and personnel working with classified electronics test equipment for aircraft. The amount of data to be examined and the number of possible faults in the network might easily have taken years to examine. By approaching the task bi-levelly, Scott intuitively found the core of the problem. The result: a forty-page report, completed in only two months, that provided information and solutions that had eluded others for two years.

A Salesman's Psychic Keys to Success

Bi-level consciousness is also effective in the person-to-person world of business. As with all things, the more skills you have available to you, the more likely you are to achieve success. John Duker, a Free Soul instructor in Washington, D.C., is the Federal accounts manager for a data communications company. Basically, he is a high-tech salesman. John's engineering background and his warm personality fit him well for the job. He adds to his success, however, by using his psychic and Soul abilities during sales calls and presentations.

John tunes in psychically before he leaves the office. He bi-levelly scans all four psychic channels, and may Soul-travel to sense his customers' specific area of interest and determine what technical data will best meet their concerns. Thus prepared, he knows exactly what materials to take along on a sales call. He also takes time to channel energy ahead for a successful meeting. If he has no appointments, John psychically searches his territory to see which clients offer the best opportunities for business that day.

When meeting with prospective clients, John Soul-shifts to sense bi-levelly how best to communicate with them, or to look for unvoiced questions or objections they may have. That way John can address concerns he would not otherwise have known existed. "This skill alone has made the difference in many sales for me," John says. "When clients see how I anticipate their needs or problems, it gives them confidence that I can provide good service. The quality of my product does the rest."

John also listens for what *not* to talk about. For example, while making a presentation to the Marine Corps for computer interfacing equipment, John intuitively sensed that he should not mention that another Marine headquarters was also interested in his product. Only later did John learn there was a personality clash between commanders at the two headquarters. Had John let each know the other was interested in his product, most likely neither would have contracted for it. Ultimately, John got both orders and the two headquarters were better served by having the same equipment.

Real estate salesperson Gail Johnston uses her Bi-level Awareness skills in her work every day. "When prospective home buyers tell me where they want to live and what kind of house they want, my multiple listing service computer normally prints out as many as one hundred homes that match the specifications," Gail says. "No client wants to take the time to inspect that many possibilities. If I don't find the 'perfect' house fairly quickly the client will go to another agent."

To ensure success, Gail shifts up to Bi-level Awareness while reviewing the multiple listings. "I am always able to select half a dozen houses I think worth investigating, and one of the group always turns out to be that 'perfect' home," says Gail. During the time she was an active real estate agent she was the top salesperson in her company, and every one of her contracts went to a satisfactory final closing.

Does using psychic and Soul potentials in business sound a bit farfetched? Not to *The Washington Post,* at any rate. In a recent article on Mind-Tapping Techniques in the Board Room, *Post* reporter Don Oldenburg featured the techniques taught by Free Soul's business division, Success Potentials Unlimited. In fact, he began his article quoting Free Soul instructor Elaine Gibbs of Fort Worth, Texas, who used her bi-level abilities as chairman of the board of a major manufacturers' representative firm: "This works in a business setting. And that's the bottom line," she says.

A Scientist Renews Her Love for Earth

Bi-level energy-blending also enhances enjoyment of your work. Suzanne Dwyier is a Ph.D. geologist with the U.S. Department of the Interior. Before her Free Soul training, Suzanne was on the verge of losing her love of her chosen lifework. The technical pressures and bureaucratic hassles involved in being one of the few senior female geologists were making Suzanne's career more stressful than enjoyable.

Bi-level blending changed all that when Suzanne started to energy-blend with the land on field trips. For years, exploring in rugged terrain had become just work that had to be done. Now the once-difficult hikes were again enjoyable walks during which she could appreciate the beauty of nature and the earth.

Further, Suzanne's bi-level psychic skills help her find the geologic samples she needs. In one instance she required only ten minutes to locate psychically the overgrown entrance to an long-abandoned small mine; she estimates it would otherwise have taken days of foot-by-foot examination of a five-square-mile area.

Using the Soul to Channel Thoughts

The Soul as energy is not merely a passive receiver; it is a transmitter as well. The more you explore your Soul, the more its energy brightens. You become a beacon radiating the caring and higher consciousness you have attained. The auras of men and women skilled in Soul-shifting reflect the heightening of their Soul energy. You can feel it when you are in their presence.

Think about the people who, when they are with you, inspire you to focus on issues of importance for humanity and leave trivial daily concerns behind. You are experiencing the touch of their heightened Soul energy, a touch that stimulates you to resonate on those same higher frequencies. This is one way spiritual leaders touch those they inspire. The radiance of their Soul energy promotes enlightenment.

The ability of the Soul to radiate consciousness-raising effects is not limited only to religious and spiritual issues. Neither is it restricted in its range or in the number of people who can be touched. Once you know how to live life as a Soul, you can broadcast positive thoughts for everyone to receive. You can channel energy to assist your life, your work, and even your community.

Transmitting a Soul Signal for Change

Richmond is a small rural community north of Detroit, with big-city problems. Fewer than four thousand people live there, yet in one six-month period in 1986 four teenagers were killed in drunk-driving accidents. A startling statistic, but not new: Richmond had seen a similar disproportionate number of these tragedies in previous years. Yet there was little demand that something be done to prevent them.

In her job as a substance-abuse prevention specialist, Barb West was responsible for organizing community groups that would initiate positive changes in local policies. But her attempts to do that job in Richmond were rebuffed. Barb was struck by the community's pervasive attitude of hopelessness. A Free Soul instructor, Barb resolved to use her Soul skills to effect a change.

In one phone conversation with a high school teacher, Barb psychically heard something that would help Richmond turn around. As the teacher described her own sense of frustration caused by the tragedy of her students' deaths and by the absence of community concern, Barb grew aware of a high-pitched tone that frequently preceded her Psychic Hearing impressions. Then she clearly heard the words, "Richmond cares." Immediately she felt an aura of confidence and conviction envelop her. She quickly repeated the phrase to the teacher and echoed it in her mind and Soul.

Barb truly did care. And she knew the vibration of caring was a psychic frequency that could be projected to reach the "caring" centers in others. Armed with nothing but this psychic slingshot, Barb resolved to take on the Goliath of Richmond's apathy. Even without initial community support she would try to change the attitude of an entire town.

Barb's first move was to organize a town meeting on behalf of the four dead youths. In her letters to the local newspaper and in her persistent telephoning she kept repeating the words, "I know Richmond cares." She not only spoke the words, she also projected them bi-levelly with every fiber of her Soul. Sixty-five people came to the first meeting. In her talk Barb continued to focus on the keyword "care." She said it repeatedly; she pulsed it from her Soul level at every opportunity. She radiated her conviction that, though she was an outsider, she knew that Richmond cared about its children.

Despite start-up problems, a citizens' committee began the task of turning around the long-standing community attitude of "What can *I* do about it?" Gradually Barb's bi-level transmissions took hold. More and more people got involved in the campaign. Barb continued to radiate the sense of caring and concern she believed existed in Richmond. Soon, news of the town's struggles spread. Executives at Detroit Edison responded to an article about the fledgling group by offering technical assistance and financial support. Those funds enabled the town to join a special substance-abuse awareness-training program.

This infusion of resources and support spurred the formation of a larger board of concerned Richmond citizens and school administrators. They sponsored a schoolwide poster contest to name their organization and promote student interest. Two youngsters submitted the winning entry— "C.A.R.E.," standing for "Caring Always Rewards Everyone." Further, Barb's original keywords were incorporated into the group's official name, "Richmond Cares." Two years later, "Richmond Cares" is still active. Through its efforts young drivers have stopped killing themselves on the rural roads of Richmond. One person *can* make a difference, particularly when she knows how to radiate on that Soul level.

Channeling a Positive Effect to the World

The benefits of radiating positive thoughts on a Soul level can even be global. Men and women around the world are using their higher consciousness to broadcast thoughts and feelings of concern for all humanity. Each new Soul voice adds to the growing chorus that calls for living in peace and harmony with our planet. As you develop your ability to Soul-shift and transmit on psychic frequencies, you, too, can aid in the evolution of world consciousness.

All too often those who take part in this New Age revolution are portrayed as "weirdos" or "kooks." Yet, as you have seen, Free Soul's students and instructors come from all walks of life, from all professions. And they represent only a fraction of the Souls working to promote a global higher consciousness. For example, Free Soul's methods have even been taught at the Pentagon to the founders of a military-civilian group spearheading a different version of SDI (the abbreviation for President Reagan's "Star Wars" program, the Strategic Defense Initiative).

Don't be alarmed. I am not referring to the use of psychic powers for military purposes, but to the Pentagon Meditation Club. Once a week in the heart of the Pentagon—in the E ring, the same ring that holds the offices of the Secretary of

Defense and the chiefs of the Armed Forces—civilian and military employees meet to project peaceful thoughts for the world. They have founded what they call "the Spiritual Defense Initiative," and are working to project a peace shield around the planet. In April 1987 I met with some of the group's leaders; later, Free Soul instructor Gerry Eitner taught club members our Soul-shifting and blending techniques.

I like to think that efforts such as this, and the global December 31 Annual Meditations for World Peace, have contributed to the recent progress in nuclear disarmament and better U.S.-Soviet relations. I know one thing for certain: Those efforts cannot hurt. When millions of people around the world actively pulse peace from a Soul level, *it has to have a positive effect.*

In the past you may have felt that one person can't make a difference, that you alone are too insignificant to make a change in the world. That time is over. From this book you have learned ways to be a pioneer at the frontier of the human potential. Already you are at the forefront of change, not only in your own life but in the lives of those around you and in the world. I encourage you with all my heart to continue exploring.

Do not let this chapter be an ending. Make it a beginning. Make it the start of your journey toward unlimitedness. Each day think of one new way to use your psychic and Soul abilities. Find ways in your daily life to practice and improve them. Create change for the better in your personal universe, and let that progress radiate outward.

In later books and through our cassette tapes and advanced retreats, Free Soul will always seek to provide a training ground for the practical and soundly motivated development of ESP and Soul potentials. Phenomena such as astral travel, past-life remembrance, energy projection, and communication with Souls on the other side are all extensions of the introductory techniques that have been presented in this book. Practice those techniques and you will be ready for the next step into the beyond far sooner than you ever dreamed possible.

Until we meet you in person—or on the Soul level in a Universe Blend Meditation—I wish you peace, happiness, and—

. . . the unlimited potentials that are your birthright as a Free Soul.

• 10 •

Answers to the 36 Most Common Questions about Psychic Phenomena

OVER THE YEARS I have found that certain questions about psychic phenomena come up over and over again. All too often these questions are derided as naive, or hostile, or ignorant. But I believe they are honest, serious, and important questions that deserve equally honest and serious answers. Here are my responses to the thirty-six questions I and other Free Soul instructors are asked most often.

1. *Why aren't laboratory experiments with ESP more successful?*

Overall, the ESP experiments carried out in the past and those currently in progress are successful. The results produced by the pioneering work of Dr. J. B. Rhine at Duke University in the early 1930s and the experimental work currently under way at Stanford Research Institute both indicate that there is substantial statistical evidence for the existence of psychic phenomena. Some of Rhine's subjects, who psychically "guessed" symbols on unseen cards, had an accuracy score twice what pure statistical chance would have yielded.

More dramatic evidence (such as the anecdotes in this book) is harder to come by in a laboratory, since a lab is a poor setting for testing psychic perception; it is nowhere near as conducive an environment for ESP as real life. If the subjects do not have a scientific background, a laboratory (with its strange equipment) can provoke counterproductive anxiety. Most of the people I tested at MIT became extremely tense under laboratory conditions. Their auras constricted; I could literally see their psychic sensitivity shutting down. Often their scores or results were statistically worse than if they had been just guessing.

Life situations are a much better setting for practicing and exploring ESP. First, people radiate energies and vibrations that are infinitely stronger than symbol cards or random-event generators (two common tools used in the laboratory to test ESP). Second, psychic vibrations never exist in a vacuum, but are interwoven with physical events. Every event carries energy on nine levels, so it simultaneously stimulates the five physical senses and the four psychic ones. Without that involvement on all nine levels, one can easily overlook or fail to identify the psychic information that completes the picture. For these reasons I urge you to explore psychic abilities in your personal laboratory of life. It's not only a more suitable environment, but your experiments can have practical applications that lead to greater success and happiness.

2. *Are women more psychic than men?*
No. Women may appear to be more psychic than men, but the apparent difference is based not so much on sex as on cultural conditioning and training. Women in our society

traditionally have been given more freedom to be feeling-oriented; the term "women's intuition" indicates our cultural bias toward allowing the possibility of psychic ability in women. On the other hand, men and, nowadays, professional women tend increasingly to be "trained out" of their psychic sensitivity. They are not encouraged to talk openly about intuition, hunches, and similar psychic impressions.

In the business community and other traditionally male-dominated fields, logic, reasoning, and analytical explanations are more respected than are feelings or intuitive hunches. Many men do indeed have flashes of psychic intuition, but usually won't present an idea as a "hunch." Women entering the business and professional world encounter the same type of psychic suppression.

Another factor that tends to help women be more open to psychic sensitivity is their experience of pregnancy and motherhood. These give women a unique opportunity to bond psychically with another Soul they cannot communicate with physically. As a result, they are more aware of the psychic frequencies. Fathers who are closely involved in rearing their children can benefit in the same way; realistically, however, mothers tend to be closer to an infant since they carry the child within their body. But both sexes can reach an equal level of psychic potential with the proper training and mental openness.

3. *In what other ways have people been trained out of their psychic abilities?*

Much of the human psychic potential is instinctive and present at Lirth. Most of that natural sensitivity atrophies as we grow up due to an overemphasis on the physical senses to the exclusion of the psychic inputs. Communicating with adults who usually listen only on physical frequencies pushes a child's psychic senses into the background. Learning to read and write requires a child to focus on physical vision and hearing, and most formal schooling provides education only in the use of our physical senses. Finally, as adults most of us receive no training or practice in developing our intuition, clairvoyance, or psychic feeling sensitivity. We are told we must be able to explain our actions logically and not rely on hunches, visions, or feelings. All of these facets combine to suppress the psychic senses until for most adults they are barely perceptible.

4. *How can I help my children not suppress their psychic ability as they grow up?*

First, communicate with them on those psychic frequencies. Before a child is born, when he or she is still an infant, and even after he or she learns to speak, make sure you keep the psychic lines open. Practice sending loving and caring feelings. Project images along with your physical directions when you teach new skills. Send a thought or voice psychically before you call a child, or start to speak and see if the youngster picks it up. There is no limit to these creative approaches. And while you are helping the child maintain his or her psychic ability, you will be rediscovering yours.

Second, do not require your child to use only rigid logic in dealing with life. Allow the expression of feelings. Do not establish a climate where an intuitive thought must be explained to be believed, or where a feeling is considered overemotional or childish. Ask what images the child sees, what dreams he or she has. Don't punish a youngster if he or she claims to hear voices or have imaginary playmates.

Third, teach children about the psychic senses. Tell them everyone has nine senses, not just five, and encourage them to use all nine. Show them the Psychic Reception Areas, tell them how to practice, and ask about their daily ESP experiences. For example, ask children if they saw the mental picture you were trying to send to them. Experiment by projecting a feeling or the words for what you want them to do *before you actually speak* the instructions. This will give you a clue as to whether they can pick up your thoughts.

Games are another possible way to teach children about the psychic senses. For example, suggest a game of psychic hide-and-seek and challenge the youngsters to use their Psychic Intuition or Psychic Feeling to help them find you. Even more effective, ask the children what games they can think of for practicing ESP. You will be amazed at how much your children can teach you.

5. *Is there ever a time that you would recommend going to a psychic reader? If so, what should I guard against?*

In general, I feel that whenever you go to someone else for a psychic reading, you are taking a step away from trusting your own abilities. A major part of developing your psychic skills is learning how to use them under difficult or stressful circumstances. Going to someone else for a reading in an emergency, or because of the importance of an issue, deprives you of the experience of operating psychically during a crucial time.

These effects can be minimized, however, if you go to a psychic reader more for confirmation than for original answers and initial information. Always tune in first yourself and see what you discover. Then, consulting a psychic reader is like getting a second and perhaps more objective opinion. Moreover, when a difficult decision must be made your psychic skills may not be as sharp as they would otherwise be. In these instances a second opinion can often provide that one piece of additional insight or, just as important, confirm the accuracy of the impression you received.

What to guard against? Obviously, look at what you are being charged. Does the reader want to be of service, or to separate you from your money? A higher fee does not necessarily mean better psychic ability or quality. A reasonable price, however, usually indicates a commitment to service and clear spiritual motives. When the psychic is reading for you or talking to you, be conscious of whether he or she is giving definitive answers to every question. All psychics have times when they simply can't get a clear signal. An honest psychic reader will tell you at least once during the interview, "I'm getting nothing on that" or "It's not completely clear." A reader who gives you an unequivocal answer to every question is probably exaggerating, and may even be making things up. Look for psychics who give you their impressions, and then try to help you sense further on your own. Most of all, beware of anyone who says, "You *must* come only to me."

6. *You talk about four personality types based on ESP strengths. Is any one of them more psychic than the others?*

Not really. Prophetics and Feelers appear to be more psychic, but that is generally because the forms of ESP that are their strengths, Psychic Intuition and Psychic Feeling, are what most people tend to think of as ESP. Visionaries and Audients seem less psychic because the way they receive ESP is closer to so-called normal thinking processes.

Psychic Intuition and Psychic Feeling also tend to be the most rapid of the psychic senses. Their impressions are immediate and distinctly separate from the physical world. Psychic Vision, because it deals in symbols, and Psychic Hearing, because it can reflect the slower process of mental understanding, usually take longer to interpret. But all four are just different ways of getting the same information. Everyone can develop the same level of psychic ability.

People high in Psychic Intuition and Psychic Feeling tend to be more naturally gifted psychically and initially more open to ESP. Their psychic strengths have characteristics that encourage the relaxed and intuitively open frame of mind that helps ESP flow freely. Those high in Psychic Vision and Psychic Hearing require a bit more training to bring out their psychic strengths. There is a natural trade-off here, however. Because Prophetics and Feelers are more naturally psychic at first, they usually find it harder to prevent psychic overload. Audients and Visionaries may need more time and practice to develop their psychic abilities, but they can claim more naturally strong and protective auras. The key is balance. Work on developing all four of your psychic gifts while at the same time increasing your auric strength.

7. *I don't want to know about bad things that are going to happen. Why should I want to be psychic?*

This viewpoint is common, but it doesn't make sense. It is based on fear rather than logic. To begin with, warnings of trouble ahead are always helpful. The future is not predetermined. If you have timely warning, any event can be altered or avoided. Even if it is too late to make a complete change of action, the warning can help you prepare for whatever difficulty may be coming. Accidents, if not preventable, can be minimized. Business setbacks can be avoided or best dealt with. If the "bad thing" sensed is the passing of a loved one, at least the warning can help you make the time remaining with that person more cherished and appreciated. The biggest sorrow I see in grief counseling is the bereaved person's feeling that he or she failed to express love and caring fully while the other person still lived.

Remember that only a small part of psychic ability deals with warnings; ESP is as easily used to sense positive opportunities. Don't think of psychic ability as just a defensive mechanism. It is equally a tool for creating your own destiny.

8. *Should I trust my psychic senses over my physical ones?*

No. The psychic senses are not there to replace your physical senses. They are there for you to work with them. Just as it is wrong to ignore the four psychic senses, it is equally unwise to follow your psychic impressions to the exclusion of physical information. The best prescription for success is to use all of your senses in making a decision.

I use my psychic senses to help me ask more of my physical senses. Thus, if I receive an ESP impression that goes counter to what my physical senses tell me, I hold off my decision. I use that psychic warning to make further physical investigations, to ask more questions, to look more deeply behind the scene. If I am unable to resolve the contradiction, I go with the stronger impression, whether it is the physical one or the psychic one. You make judgments like this all the time, comparing contradictory evidence of your physical senses. For example, if an item of food looked tasty but smelled bad, you probably wouldn't eat it. Or you would taste it to get a third impression. If it also tasted bad, you wouldn't eat it no matter how good it looked. The same type of reasoning applies to the use of your psychic senses. No responsible ESP educator would encourage you to follow your psychic impressions exclusively and ignore your physical senses.

Just because you get a bad feeling about, say, an electrical appliance you want to buy, don't cancel the purchase altogether. See if a different time for buying feels better to you; compare the item with other brands to see if you can find a better product, or lower price. Similarly, if you have an "off" feeling about an airline flight, don't assume that you should give up your trip. Rather, look for a different flight, a better connection, a different departure time. You may just be picking up the impression that the original flight may be delayed or have problems with baggage. Not every psychic impression involves physical danger.

Responding to negative impressions about people, rather than objects, requires a somewhat different approach. Say you are getting nagging negative images and feelings about a babysitter, or an employee, and cannot get such feelings out of your mind. In that case find out if the person is under temporary stress or if other people have had consistent and similar problems with them. In short, use your psychic skills to set in motion and complement your wise use of physical investigation.

9. *Why do most people fail when they try to be psychic?*
They try too hard. They are forcing and overconcentrat-

ing—habits that lock you into your *physical* senses. Psychic perception requires a more relaxed *mental* state: a focused awareness, not a forced one. In addition, most people do not know where the Psychic Reception Areas are or how to tap them. As a result, they lack the three catalysts essential for ESP: (1) They don't have a way to increase the strength of psychic signals; (2) they don't have a focal point to switch on ESP; (3) most important, they don't have a way to practice and improve. The Psychic Reception Areas are the keys that make ESP accessible to everyone.

10. *Are the Psychic Reception Areas the same as the chakras?*

No. They are two separate entities. Psychic Reception Areas are focal points for the psychic senses when you sense through the physical body. The chakras are the energy centers of the spiritual body. Many Eastern religions and metaphysical philosophies consider the chakras to be those points where vitalizing energy flows into our physical body from the Soul's etheric or astral body. The only connection between the chakras and the Psychic Reception Areas is that some of their locations are similar. For example, the Feeling Psychic Reception Area is located in the same area as the solar plexus and the abdominal chakras. The Intuition Psychic Reception Area is in the same general location as the crown, or inflow chakra. The Vision Psychic Reception Area is close to the chakras associated with the pineal and pituitary glands. Though these locations are similar, the functions of the two systems are quite different. As a physical analogy, consider that though the esophagus and the windpipe are both in the throat area, it would be a serious error to say they are the same, or related in any way save by their proximity.

11. *Are the Russians ahead of us in psychic testing and development?*

It may be possible that the Russians are further along in

the actual testing of psi phenomena, but there is no doubt in my mind that they are significantly behind America in the development of psychic abilities and in methods for teaching psychic potential. Everything psi-oriented requires relaxation and inner calm to be successful. Those attitudes and states of mind are hard to maintain in a repressive regime. Two of our Free Soul instructors, Zhanna and Ilya Kalinovsky, emigrated from the Soviet Union. They have shared stories with me about how their friends were persecuted and, in some cases, jailed for attempting to teach even yoga classes. Ilya and Zhanna wept when they first heard about Free Soul. That training like ours could be so accessible to the public seemed miraculous to them.

This difference in the freedom between the two societies is, I believe, what puts Americans decades ahead of the Soviet Union in the development of psychic potential on a national level. What really determines true advantage in any situation is the core level of training of a nation's people. Whether that training involves literacy and technical abilities or increased ESP and psychic strength, free people will always make better progress. As a people's level of extrasensory ability increases, their psychic defenses also strengthen.

12. *Can someone use psychic powers to control me?*
Absolutely not. While it is true that someone with strong psychic abilities (particularly those of thought projection) can influence or put pressure on you, the ESP frequencies are too subtle to create the "mind-control" effects many people fear. It has been demonstrated conclusively that even under hypnosis you cannot be made to do anything contrary to your moral code, inner desire, or choice. If you are ambivalent about a decision, and someone around you strongly favors a certain point of view, then, yes, sometimes psychic suggestion can tip the balance in that direction. It cannot, however, make you do something you're not already open to.

Moreover, most people have a natural psychic defense against extrasensory pressures. It's a kind of psychic rebellion reflex. Even people who know nothing about ESP tend to tense up under strong psychic pressures from outside. If anything, that reflexive tightening leads to indecision or rebellion rather than acquiescence. Just as an attempt at physical persuasion frequently backfires, so too psychic pressuring usually fails to work.

It *is* possible for someone to confuse and disorient you psychically. Any type of psychic bombardment is disruptive and can interfere with your thinking and your performance. But it would be wrong to believe that psychic interference can extend to outright control. Learning to develop your own ESP abilities is the best defense against psychic pressure. Once you learn the Psychic Reception Areas and how to turn on your psychic sensitivity at will, you will also know how to turn it off. Then you can reduce your receptivity to vibrations on those channels. You can also learn to adjust your aura to deflect any psychic pressures. In our courses we teach several different methods for strengthening the aura and repelling psychic attack.

13. *How can I tell if a feeling is a psychic warning or just my own inner fears?*

The best way to tell the difference between a valid Psychic Feeling warning and a personal fear is to note the exact location of your impression. A Psychic Feeling signal will usually be experienced mainly in the solar plexus or abdominal region. This is what's commonly referred to as having butterflies or a "sinking" feeling in the pit of the stomach. A fear that is *not* based on a psychic warning will usually stimulate an adrenalin-triggered fight-or-flight physiological reaction. Adrenalin makes your heart race, shortens your breathing, and raises your blood pressure. The overall effect is a sensation of tightness and tension in the upper chest that is distinct from the "gut" feeling.

14. *How can I screen out feelings I don't want to receive?*

Primarily by realizing that you are psychic and that some of the feelings you have may not be yours. This mental awareness of your psychic receptivity can often sharply reduce the negative effect of feelings you are picking up from other people. You can protect yourself even further by specifically identifying the person from whom the negative feelings are coming. Knowing these two things helps to place the signal outside of yourself and prevents you from accepting and magnifying it.

If you must stay in an environment where people are radiating unpleasant feelings, try to sit in such a way that your Feeling Psychic Reception Area faces away from them. Turn sideways when you are dealing with them, or position your chair or desk so their energy strikes you glancingly rather than head-on. If you must deal with that person face-to-face, cover your abdominal region with your arms in the instinctual crossed-arm body language that protects your Feeling Psychic Reception Area. Getting behind a desk (especially a wooden one) also helps. Putting that extra layer of energy-absorbent material between you and the sender can reduce the intensity of the feelings you receive.

15. *Why don't all premonitions and intuitive hunches come true?*

Psychic Intuition, or any premonition, can only tune in to possibilities. The future is not fixed. There are, in fact, many possible futures. A hunch or premonition is a way of psychically sensing the probability that a particular event will occur. Your own actions or the actions of others subsequent to your premonition will affect what develops. Most minor problems you have hunches about can be avoided if you take corrective measures. Premonitions that come true are usually cases where the precognitive person was powerless to make a difference.

Here we see the main reason why prophecy and premonition are the hardest psychic phenomena to prove scientifically. Who would want, for the sake of satisfying some skeptic, to allow a disaster to occur if they could prevent it? I would rather you prove your psychic abilities to yourself by avoiding problems instead of allowing them to develop. Wouldn't you?

16. *How can I tell if an intuitive impression is a valid premonition, or if I am only psychically picking up the thoughts of people around me? Can I merely be sensing what they want me to do or wish to happen?*

The key is whether the impression occurs only in the presence of those other people. Get out of their immediate vicinity and see if your intuitive knowing is still as strong. The thoughts of others can be picked up at a distance, but the signal is not usually as strong. If your impression weakens when you are alone, you were probably picking up other people's thoughts or expectations. For this reason it is always wise to make your final decisions in a clear space where you can be alone.

17. *How can I tell the difference between Psychic Hearing and talking to myself?*

Psychic Hearing is frequently mistaken for talking to yourself because both use the same internal circuitry of the brain's temporal lobes. To tell the difference, notice where your perception of the sound originates. When you talk to yourself, your perception of the answering voice will usually tend to be on your left side, in the left-brain area, because this is the part of the brain that deals with language and language formation. Some people, particularly left-handers, notice the impression more on the right side. Which side really doesn't matter, however. The main difference between talking to yourself and Psychic Hearing impressions is that the latter seem to occur more in the center of your head.

Also, the clairaudient impression will not necessarily be heard in your own voice. It will be a word, a phrase, or language that's understood in a generic voice. When you talk to yourself, your answers are likely to be more in your own tone of voice and your personal speaking style.

18. *I don't normally have Psychic Hearing experiences, but I have had one or two that were quite striking and loud. What does that mean?*

This apparent contradiction is a common experience. Psychic Hearing seems to be the least developed psychic sense for most people. Probably because it is so close to that inner mental dialogue, we tend to tune it out or fail to recognize it. As a result, it has atrophied or been suppressed. You actually have many minor Psychic Hearing experiences throughout your day; but if you consider them as talking to yourself, you may not recognize how sensitive to Psychic Hearing you are.

A signal that is striking, dangerous, or urgent enough to be at full volume catches your attention. You remember it. Having that single, full-volume Psychic Hearing experience often leads to the misconception that *all* clairaudient impressions must be loud to be valid. As a result you continue to ignore the subtler forms of Psychic Hearing that you are constantly receiving.

19. *Are mental telepathy, thought transference, mind reading, and thought projection all the same thing? What psychic senses do they involve?*

All four refer to the transmission of information between two people by means other than the five physical senses. They are different terms for psychic communication between minds. In general, thought transference and thought projection refer to the sending phenomena; mind reading and mental telepathy refer to receiving. It would be incorrect to assume that because its impressions come in words and language form, Psychic Hearing is the type of ESP most linked with thought transference, thought projection, mind reading, and mental telepathy. These psychic transfers can occur with any of the four psychic senses.

People high in Psychic Intuition are usually better at mind reading and mental telepathy because they are the most receptive. Intuitive people "know" what the other person is thinking; because Psychic Intuition is the quickest of the four senses it is able to grasp and comprehend fleeting thoughts. Feelings and pictures can be communicated just as easily, but they are harder to interpret.

People naturally strong in Psychic Hearing usually make the best transmitters for thought projection or thought transference. Thinking in words makes a psychic signal radiate louder and thus it is easier to pick up. People high in Psychic Feeling are the best at a cross between mind reading and mental telepathy—you might call it "mood reading." They more readily sense when something is wrong with another person. Those high in Psychic Vision can be best at seeing people's thoughts or mood reflected in their auras.

20. *How can I interpret the symbolism in Psychic Vision?*

The best key for interpreting the symbols of Psychic Vision is to use the other psychic senses. If Psychic Feeling is easy for you, ask, "What does it feel like it means?" If you are high in Psychic Intuition, ask, "What do I know it means?" If you are a more Audient person, ask, "What seems to make sense logically; what do I understand from mental associations with that symbol?" All clairvoyant images and dreams come interwoven with intuitions, feelings, and understandings. Learn to trust the supporting impressions you receive through the other psychic senses, and your interpretation will usually be right.

21. *Do all people see the same type of clairvoyant images?*

No! If you are high in Psychic Intuition, frequently you will see "flash" pictures—fleeting images you may not be able to hold for long on your mental screen. This is natural for you. Don't try to slow down the images. Trying to force them to stay will block your Psychic Vision and you will end up seeing nothing. Instead, grasp the image quickly and trust your impressions. If you want confirmation, it is better to get the image to reflash than to try to hold on to the original picture.

If you are high in Psychic Feeling, the images you see may be slightly blurred or muted (like impressionist art). This is natural for you. To clarify them, use the feelings you sense from the images rather than trying to force a crisp picture.

If you are an Audient, your clairvoyant images may look more like mental schematics or blueprints. You may understand the pictures' meaning better than you see them. Don't be distressed if you do not receive the same type of panoramic images that some Visionaries do. *Trust that the way you understand your inner view is accurate for you.*

22. *What psychic sense is best for planning?*

All of the psychic senses should be used in planning, but Psychic Vision is best for integrating the overall plan. It can help you see all the factors involved in your final decision-making. Future planning impressions will often come to you through intuition and prophecy. Psychic Feeling can give you an accurate "feel" for the fine points of the plan. Using the mental understanding that goes with your Audient side will help you stay organized to better accomplish your goal. As a final step, tap your Psychic Vision to let you see the big picture. Vision helps you integrate your plan by taking into account its different aspects. To tap Psychic Vision in planning, visualize all the facets of the plan and then feel, know, or understand (based on your strengths) what needs changing or adjusting.

23. *How does practicing visualization improve clairvoyance and Aura Vision?*

Both Psychic Vision and visualization use the same inner screen of the "third eye." When you practice visualization you are adjusting the clarity of that inner screen. With that improved focus, all your visual psychic impressions will be clearer, whether they are clairvoyant visions or Aura Visions.

It is also important to learn the difference between an image you are creating mentally and one that is a valid psychic perception. The more you practice visualization, the more you learn to recognize the feel of the pictures you are drawing with your mind. That familiarity in turn helps you to recognize a psychic vision when it comes because you will sense your lack of control over shaping its image.

24. *Why doesn't everyone see the same thing when looking at a person's aura?*

This is a reasonable question, and it raises an issue that leads skeptics to deny the validity of Aura Vision. What their criticism fails to take into account is the complexity of the aura. The aura has many facets and layers, and consists of several interlocking energy fields. Thus it is never a single color or a constant image; it changes from moment to moment.

The main reason we don't all see the same image when looking at one specific aura is that each viewer is tuning in to a different aspect or layer of the aura. In addition, each person sees the image through the prism of their own aura. It's not so much that one's own aura biases the colors one sees, but that it directs one's psychic attention to a specific layer or facet of the subject's aura. Moreover, each person has more than just one or two personality attributes or characteristics; thus it would be foolish to assume that his or her aura would have only one color. Remember the story of the seven blind men who described an elephant differently based on which part of the animal they felt? So too different people will psychically see different facets of the same aura.

The bottom line in Aura Vision is not so much exactly what is seen, but how it is interpreted. All Psychic Vision is at times symbolic. Each of you has his or her own symbol system and color associations. That two people describe the same colors and patterns is not as important as reaching the same general interpretation of the color patterns they see.

25. *Is there any color in the aura that is bad or evil, or that I am right to be afraid of seeing?*

Black is the color most often associated with negative aspects in an aura. It is not a color to fear seeing, however. In fact, it appears frequently in most auras, and usually signifies pressure or tension. It is definitely not an automatic indication of evil, or something to fear. Many people mistakenly think a black aura indicates death or the approach of death. This is incorrect. Actually, it is the *absence* of color, or the *absence* of the aura itself, that signifies the approach of death.

The location of black in the aura is also an important factor. Black over a particular physical area of the body indicates surgery, illness, or some type of constriction or dysfunction in that location. Black that appears around the body or on the sides of the aura usually indicates tension in the individual's environment—and more often this refers to thoughts directed at the person rather than his or her own negativity. Even black around the head is not necessarily a sign of evil. Most of the time it means only that the person is under tremendous pressure. That tension compresses the energy field so that it cannot blossom into full color.

Never be afraid of what you see in an aura. See it, sense for an interpretation, and then apply the interpretation in the most helpful and practical way.

26. *What distance should I keep between myself and other people to protect my aura from being infringed upon?*

It depends on who you are with and on your cultural and psychic training. The boundary of the aura is flexible and is keyed to your concept of personal space. The aura can adjust almost instantaneously to changing circumstances as long as you allow it to do so. People who have to ride on crowded subways or buses learn out of necessity how to pull their auras in and prevent invasion of their personal space. Some cultures accept and even expect close physical contact. In these cases an inner boundary is maintained while the outer aura may encompass or wrap around those close by.

Find a distance that feels comfortable and work to stabilize it. At times that may mean keeping people at a specific physical distance; at other times it may mean expanding or shrinking your aura. Learning to make these adjustments isn't difficult; simply hold in mind the thought of how you want your aura to be. Working with setting your aura boundary can also be beneficial. In some situations I find that a strong and solid boundary gives me the greatest protection. In others, letting the boundary be flexible and pliable, so it will bend but not break, is the better approach. Shaping your aura like a wedge, so that pressures are deflected around you, is also a good solution.

27. *Is it better to maintain a wide aura for increased psychic sensitivity, or to keep it tight for increased protection?*

This question reflects a basic misconception about the aura. Psychic sensitivity and psychic protection are not directly linked to the width of the aura. Many people think a wide aura is automatically more psychically sensitive and thus more vulnerable. This leads them to believe that to protect themselves psychically they need to pull in their aura.

Here is what actually happens: Pulling your aura in temporarily increases boundary strength, condensing and solidifying its energy into a more effective shield that provides a momentary increase in psychic protection. But this concentration of the aura eventually causes you to become tense and irritable. The more this happens, the less freely spiritual energy flows to the aura. As a result its strength actually starts to diminish until the aura collapses, leaving you totally vulnerable.

The best technique is to expand the aura—but with strength. Free Soul teaches a variety of methods for charging and strengthening the aura so that, as it expands, the outer boundary remains strong and resilient. This gives you increased sensitivity plus increased protection.

Having a wide aura does not automatically make a person vulnerable. Most people with wide auras are vulnerable only because they don't know the Psychic Reception Areas. When you know the four locations you can switch your psychic sensitivity off when you want to be protected. People who do not understand this think that to be more psychic, they must stay open and attuned all the time. But that overopenness is what expands the aura too far and makes them vulnerable.

28. *Does that mean that expanding my consciousness through Soul-blending can also make me vulnerable?*

No. The boundary of the aura and the Soul's degree of blendedness are separate functions. When the aura is too wide without being suitably strong, people do become vulnerable to psychic energies around them. If they live or work in a tense or pressured environment they then more easily pick up other people's negative feelings, tensions, and depressions. But when you energy-blend as a Soul you harmonize with the object or environment you are blending with. It is a sensation of oneness rather than vulnerability. And the natural harmony of Soul-blending can counteract many of the negative vibrations to which you may be exposed.

It is wise, however, to do blending meditations in a positive environment, or at least one that you can control to some degree. Blending in the middle of a rush-hour crowd or in a hostile environment is not sensible. Until you develop more control over blending, it is best to have at the minimum your own bubble of space while you are extending.

29. *What is to keep frequent experiences of universe-blending from causing a loss of my identity?*

There is no danger of losing your identity in practicing the Universe Blend Meditation (as described in Chapter 8). If anything, you only enhance and deepen it. The purpose of the Universe Blend Meditation is to help you realize how much a part of all things you already are, not to dissolve or diminish your unique consciousness. When properly done, the Universe Blend Meditation gives you a sense of being one with everything, but still maintains your sense of identity.

This physical analogy may help illustrate how you can expand your consciousness yet retain your uniqueness. Picture one red blood-cell traveling through the circulatory system looking for "the Body." Everywhere the blood cell goes it questions other cells. It asks the muscle cells, "Have you seen the Body? Do you know where it is?" It asks the bone and ligament cells: "Do you know how I can find the Body?" Each in turn responds, "No, we're just doing our work supporting, contracting, connecting." Even the brain's nerve cells can't tell the red blood cell where to find "the Body." Finally the blood cell realizes that *every* cell is a part of the Body; that the Body *is* the cells and that cells are, each in its unique way, the Body.

Like our body's cells, each of us is part of a greater whole, a part of the All. The energy and atoms that comprise you have existed since the beginning of time. If, as science believes, the universe as we know it was created in the primeval Big Bang, then the energy and matter compressed in that cosmic egg is still linked, even though expanding outward. Tapping the Universe Blend Meditation helps you to feel and experience that linkage. It helps you to connect with the spiritual family you have throughout the universe. It helps you raise your consciousness to higher levels.

30. *What is meant by the phrase "akashic records," and how does it pertain to psychic perception?*

The akashic record (or records) is an expression used in metaphysics to describe the storage of all information. The idea that everything is recorded is true. Science tells us that every ray of light that has ever shone is still shining somewhere in the universe. The same is true of all types of vibration. The misconception is that these data are stored in a kind of psychic library in some corner of the galaxy, encrypted on crystal tapes kept in a mystical spiritual vault.

Every event, thought, interaction, or desire radiates a complex series of energies and frequencies that are still resonating somewhere. We don't have the technology to ascertain if that "somewhere" is in the far reaches of space or in a different dimension. You can tune in to them, however, through the Soul and the psychic senses. This is why you can sense into the past. Each time you use your psychic ability to review in retrospect you are, in a sense, tapping a small section of the akashic records.

31. *How does* déjà vu *work? What psychic senses are involved?*

Déjà vu, French for "already seen," is a term frequently applied to different types of ESP experience. In psychic terms it has come to mean an impression that you have been in a certain place before, or have previously seen a certain situation or person. That impression can come through any of the four psychic senses: It can be a feeling, a knowing, an understanding, or a clairvoyant visual recognition.

The explanation for a *déjà vu* sensation varies according to the situation. Sometimes it is a result of being in an area that has a psychic energy pattern similar to a place familiar to you. Another explanation is that you have Soul-traveled, or remote-viewed that location before, either in your sleep or subconsciously. People high in Psychic Intuition get a prophetic knowing about circumstances and people coming their way; thus when they encounter that situation or person later, they have the *déjà vu* sensation. Reincarnation—having lived in a place or with a person in a previous life—is another frequently proposed explanation.

How do you determine which of these explanations is correct for your particular *déjà vu* experience? Use your psychic sensitivities to determine which feels most accurate and appropriate. Which one makes the most sense? Nine times out of ten your interpretation will be right.

32. *Is it possible to heal everything using the mind?*
Yes and no. While nerve connections do exist to every part of the body, whether "everything" can be healed with mind-body control is determined by other factors. Time, skill, and discipline play equally important roles. Early detection of an illness or dysfunction can be crucial to the effectiveness of your self-healing abilities. The skill with which you tap the involuntary nerve networks and stimulate your immune system is another determining factor. So is the extent to which you are willing to practice and apply what you know. You must judge for yourself how these three factors apply in your particular case. Nowhere, however, is it appropriate to use mind-body self-healing to the exclusion of other forms of medicine. Weave all forms of treatment together into a holistic approach to the problem.

Whether to use mind-body control to heal a specific dysfunction is also a question of priorities. Is it worth the time it would take? Do I believe you can correct hay fever or nearsightedness using mind-body control? Yes, I do. Is it worth the time in most cases? No, it's not. It's far simpler to wear glasses and put the time into more important areas—

your family, your work, your spiritual quest for enlightenment.

Don't make the state of your physical health a measure of
your self-worth. Remember, you are a Soul that has a body.
You are not the body. Place your emphasis on Soul health
and wholeness rather than on physical perfection. As you get
older it's natural for the body to deteriorate physically. Use
your self-healing skills to alleviate the effects of the aging
process, but do not make physical perfection the main standard by which you measure yourself. If you do, you'll fall
victim to a spiritual form of vanity, and miss the whole point
of being a Soul.

33. *Is there any danger in interfering with the body's
automatic regulatory systems, such as blood pressure and
pulse?*

None whatsoever. Mental attempts to enhance health so
far have shown only positive results. The body's automatic
regulatory systems are so deeply and firmly established that
there is no danger of permanently altering them in a harmful
way.

In many respects our body is an evolutionary antique, still
geared to protect us from physical dangers that for the most
part no longer exist. Our caveman ancestors needed the
surge of adrenalin that the fight-or-flight response provided
when they were faced with predators that could eat them
alive. Today's threats and stresses do not require this heightened physical reaction. If anything, increased calmness and
clear thinking are the keys to survival and success. Unfortunately, our body has not changed as rapidly as the times.
When the mind sends stress signals, the body overreacts.
Whatever you can do to reduce this stress reflex can only
help prevent physical wear and tear.

34. *What can I do to avoid the danger of getting lost
when Soul-shifting—of not being able to get back into the
body?*

There is no danger at all. You may not realize it but you Soul-shift and Soul-travel every day either through daydreams or at night during sleep. Multiply your age by 365 and you'll have a rough idea of how many times you have already Soul-shifted without the least difficulty in getting back.

This question probably arises out of descriptions in psychic magazines of people who experienced astral projection or out-of-the-body travel, and had trouble returning to the body. These experiences are not fabrications or exaggerations; they do happen. But they are more a result of panic than of inherent danger. Someone who has never experienced controlled Soul-shifting or out-of-the-body travel may well become frightened and spiritually freeze. That terror prevents the natural return of the consciousness to the body.

In Chapter 8, the process you learned for ending the Soul-shift (bringing your focus back into the head area, feeling some part of your face, gently moving a finger or a foot, and opening your eyes when you feel comfortable) teaches you the basics for ensuring return. Accounts of people who had trouble returning after an out-of-the-body experience usually end the same way, with the person finally being able to move a finger or blink an eye. After you practice the Soul-shift several times, moving into and out of an enhanced Soul state is no riskier than getting in and out of a chair.

35. *What psychic sense works best for out-of-the-body experiences?*

Traveling out of the body is an extension of the Soul skill of shifting consciousness. The psychic senses have nothing to do with it. They come into play only to help you navigate and perceive once you are already out. Which psychic sense is better for perceiving on the Soul level varies from person to person, depending on your psychic strengths. The important thing is to use the form of sensing you feel most comfortable with, and to realize that each has its own characteristics.

If you are stronger in Psychic Feeling, don't expect to see

as many images, or to look down at your body. It is more realistic for you to be in tune on a feeling level than to actually see. Since you will often be viewing from a different dimension, even a person high in Psychic Vision will find the images unlike those he or she sees with physical eyes. Expect that difference; get used to it.

36. *Is there any limit to how far I can go in my exploration of psychic ability and Soul consciousness?*

The only limitations will be the ones you allow. Your true nature is to be unlimited. The more you search, the more you will find. At Free Soul's advanced courses and retreats you will discover that the more you learn, the more you will encounter new ways to explore further. Free Soul's ultimate aim is to help you learn to be your own teacher.

The best spiritual master for determining your life's path and quest is yourself. No one else knows your needs, your past, or your life purposes better. Seek to find your own truth and you will learn how never to be without answers. The universe will become your playground. You will achieve the unlimited potentials that are your birthright as a Free Soul.

Index